Alterations
To A Life Jacket

Alterations To A Life Jacket

TALES OF A YOUNG MAN'S SURVIVAL

A memoir by
FRANK MAROTTA

Copy-edited by Jackie Sherbow

DISCLAIMER: Some statements are of the author's opinion. They are not an assertation based solely on fact. The conversations come from the author's recollections of certain events. They are not written to represent word for word transcripts, but rather retold in a manner that evokes the feelings and memories in the way they were said. The specific timelines, locations, and actual events are factual. Some names have been changed to protect the identity of the individuals. The publisher makes no claims as to their veracity or accuracy and assumes no liability for the content.

Author would like to thank Michael Ferrara Photography and Jackie Sherbow Editing

Charleston, SC
www.PalmettoPublishing.com

Alterations To A Life Jacket

Copyright © 2021 by Frank Marotta

All rights reserved.

No portion of this book may be reproduced, stored in a retrieval system, or transmitted in any form by any means—electronic, mechanical, photocopy, recording, or other—except for brief quotations in printed reviews, without prior permission of the author.

First Edition

Paperback ISBN: 978-1-63837-156-4
eBook ISBN: 978-1-63837-157-1

To my Frank Jr. and Tanyanelle: With a great abundance of sincere love, respect, and gratitude. For your continued valiant display of perseverance you showed at an early age, dealing with life-altering circumstances that were out of your control and no fault of your own, I commend you. I will never forget. You both exemplify the meaning of respect, as you both have become humble, caring adults, along with being exceptional parents and role models for your children and my grandchildren.

To your mother, for always doing her absolute best in raising the both of you as a single parent, I am forever grateful.

To my beautiful and wonderful granddaughters Leah Rose, Emma Grace, Rosemary Cecelia, and Helen Paloma: Though you are far away in other states, you all remain deeply close to my heart.

To my two new grandsons, Roman Francis and Vincent Jason who have given us all so much love, joy, and laughter. We are fortunate to have you in the same state. When you all call me "Grampy," it still melts my heart all the time.

To my Grandmother Tessie: You were always my guiding light and shining star in an otherwise dark childhood. Thank you for telling me about my Italian heritage, for teaching me the language, for always being there for me. For showing me life lessons that I still live by today. I was extremely fortunate to have you so close both physically and emotionally. Could not have imagined life without you growing up. Gram, you will forever remain in my heart. With everlasting love.

Contents

FOREWORD ix
INTRODUCTION xiii
I   MOMMY DEAREST & OUR DYSFUNCTION JUNCTION 1
II   A QUEEN'S CROWN 6
III THE QUEST TO LEAVE THE NEST 17
IV YOU MAKE ME FEEL BRAND NEW 24
V   GOODBYE MACARONI & MEATBALLS, HELLO RICE & BEANS ... 29
VI A NEW WIFE, A NEW LIFE & HERE COMES THE SON 34
VII THE NIGHTS THE LIGHTS WENT OUT IN THE BIG APPLE 42
VIII FAREWELL TO OUR GENTLE GIANT 48
IX A DETECTIVE & THE BREAKDOWN AT EXIT 17 53
X   NO STOMACH FOR THE WORLD OF THE BULLS & THE BEARS .. 61
XI HISTORY REPEATS ITSELF & YOU'RE NOT MY FATHER 68
XII GOT A JOB IN A WOMEN'S WORLD & THE BEES WERE A BUZZIN' .. 72
XIII MR. MOM CONTINUES TO MANAGE IT ALL 77
XIV MY PATIENCE AT HOME CONTINUED TO DEPLETE & MY PATIENTS AT WORK WERE COMPLETELY DEPLETED 83
XV SCIENCE & RELIGION IN THE FACE OF POSSIBLE LIFE AND DEATH· 87
XVI A STALKER, A CRUCIAL DECISION & MOMMY DEAREST MAKES A COMEBACK 92
XVII TURNING OVER A NEW LEAF & ON MY WAY TO A MEDICAL PROFESSION 98
XVIII AN OFFICIAL ENDING, AN OFFICIAL BEGINNING, AN OFFICIAL TITLE 103
XIX A QUEENS TALE: FROM A LAB COAT TO A BLUE COLLAR 107
ACKNOWLEDGEMENTS 119
EPILOGUE 123
ABOUT THE AUTHOR 127

FOREWORD

When Frank Marotta asked me to write this foreword, I was rather surprised but very honored. My career is in video production and event videography. As for my writing skills, I wish I was more confident. As I will address this memoir, my thoughts and feelings about my dear friend Frank Marotta are presented with the utmost truth, coming directly from my heart and soul.

I had the pleasure of meeting Frank over the phone through a mutual friend a few years ago. We were about to embark on a film project, a documentary about our beloved hometown of Corona, Queens. Frank was an associate producer and I did sound, lighting and filming. We greeted each other on the phone and he asked if I knew him or the Marotta family; he said he knew my brother Ralph and my father Corky, as well as many mutual friends from the neighborhood. He seemed to have known everyone and everything about Corona.

From our brief conversation over the phone and reminiscing about Corona, I immediately took a liking to him. I had that feeling that I'd known him all my life. I looked forward to meeting him in person. I did not know what he looked like, but as we spoke I started to paint a mental picture of him, as he sounded like a very pleasant and knowledgeable guy. I pictured a composite of the many Italian-American men I knew in Corona.

Our initial meeting, a few years ago when we discussed the documentary, was set for Tony's Pizzeria on 104th Street in Corona. A Corona landmark. As he sat there, he was nothing like what I had pictured. He was larger than me, stocky, very imposing, clean shaven (both face and head). He had striking green eyes. He also had sort of a celebrity aura that surrounded him. Just a few months ago, Frank told me his intentions on writing his memoir. I was both excited and supportive. We would continue to have many phone conversations. They would consist of shared interests about our beloved Corona, history, politics, current events, family values, and Italian-American traditions. I'm not so much interested in sports, but I respected Frank's vast knowledge of them. He even had a tryout with the Cincinnati Reds, which you will hear about in the book. He would often tell me stories of people and events in his life that I always found interesting and entertaining and that he wanted to put in a memoir.

Over the next few weeks, he would tell me of his progress in writing this memoir. When he finally finished, he sent me the manuscript. I read it with great enthusiasm. I was interested in seeing him succeed. I knew some of the many tales, people, and events that it would convey. I found that there was something much more profound and deeper than those stories.

So you may ask, "Who really is this person Frank Marotta, and why did I read his memoir when he is not a known person—not a celebrity of movies, TV, or media, not a captain of industry or business, and not a politician or statesman?"

Because this, my friends, is the story of a common man. Not the common man very often maligned in the literature and philosophy of cultural elites that is looked down upon as unrefined and indolent, but the common man who is the unsung hero, who endures life with all its ups and downs, trials and tribulations, twists and turns, failures and successes. The common man who seeks to improve his lot in life with hard work and education.

The common man who takes care of his family the best way he knows how, the common man who deals with the illnesses and deaths of loved ones. The common man battling the slings and arrows of life searching for his peaceful, comfortable niche which leads him to where he's supposed to be. Grounded in a fulfilled life, loved and respected by family, friends, and associates.

It may be the movers and shakers of the world and the captains of industry, business, media, and government who get most of the recognition in this life, but they would not exist without the common man laboring, buying and selling, paying his share to society, raising a good family, and being a good neighbor and friend. You could look for him in mythology, movies, or works of philosophy and literature—but he is closer than you thought, for he is Frank Marotta. The Common Man. The true Atlas who holds up the celestial spheres.

Michael Ferrara

INTRODUCTION

*H*i! How ya doin'? Let me introduce myself. My name is Francis Marotta. Pleased to meet ya. Before I go any further, I have to tell you something. You see, that's not my real first name. Well, maybe it is. I had the pleasure to come into this world on a hot summer day in July of 1954, on a Monday, to be exact. Right after the special delivery that my mother—Rosie—got, her nurse asked her if she had a name ready for her beautiful blond baby boy. She said yes.

"Okay," the nurse replied. "What is it?" My mother said, "*Frank*." The nurse answered, in a quizzical tone, "Wait a minute, aren't you Roman Catholic?" Ma answered, "Of *course!*" "Don't you know, asked the nurse, "you're supposed to name your child after a *saint?*" Ma's answer was, "Not really," and the nurse's advice was, "Well, if you are a good Catholic, I suggest you change *Frank* to *Francis*." Ma agreed.

Now, the funny part is that, in my entire life, I have never been called Francis. Frank mostly; Frankie by my family and friends.

Growing up, there were three Franks in the house. My father and my grandfather were the other two. As I got older, when someone in the house said "Hey, Frank," the three of us turned around at the same time. It always got a laugh.

I was Rosie and Big Frank's third and youngest child at the time. It was Anthony, MaryAnne, then me. They would go on to have three more, for a grand total of six. There's research that says a middle sibling does indeed face challenges that the others don't. Some psychological and other distinct personality issues will arise. These traits can follow an individual well into his adulthood. Believe me, they did. I must say some were good, some were bad.

My mother was known by few names. Rose Mary, Rose Marie, Rosie, Ro, Ro Ro. She would also have a few different personalities that only her kids witnessed. She was abusive to all of us on many levels. Rosie was also oblivious to the dysfunctional household she was creating. She was the "model mother" on the outside. Behind closed doors, it was a different story. Raising six kids in a two-bedroom apartment was a major factor that contributed to her instabilities. You can also add in obsessive-compulsive disorder issues.

Now, getting back to me: It wasn't till I was nineteen that I had my first real girlfriend. You could say I was a late bloomer, and I will explain that later on. Her name was Carmen. She was from Puerto Rico. She was also eleven years older than me, had two girls (nine and ten years old), and had been separated for eight years from her husband. I knew that was a whole bunch of baggage to carry at the time, and I knew there would be no way in hell that my parents would ever accept a relationship looking like that.

I would have to keep this all a secret from them as long as I could. I knew I would eventually have to face the music. I also believed I was facing a sort of identity crisis. I was stuck between being too old to being an actual kid and too young to being a man, crazy as it sounds.

When I was twenty-one, Carmen told me she was pregnant with our child. In those days the term "a baby out of wedlock" carried an extremely large stigma. My morals, my scruples, my DNA just told me the right thing to do was to marry her. I really did not know any better. On November 5, 1975, we were married in a civil ceremony. I knew what I would have to face. It would not be easy. I was very determined to make it all work. That is what I hoped for.

Was I trying to escape and break down the walls of dysfunction and abuse I had been subjected to over the years? Was I looking for a mother figure? You will have to be the judge and the jury. These many issues and emotions have been locked up inside me much too long. Writing this has been quite cathartic.

So now I take you on my journey. I will be your tour guide. I promise you candor as you step into the spaces of my mind, body, and soul. You will hear, feel, and touch faith, hope, charity, depression, oppression, racism, guilt, the celebration of life, the sorrows of death, the plight of dreams, some sexual content. Above all, the everlasting spirit of survival. My journey will take you from 1964 to 1985. You will feel the essence of most of the years I will be referring to. I will also be addressing some of the popular cultural history lessons along the way.

I welcome you aboard my roller coaster. The ups and downs, the twists and turns, the ins and outs. It will all take your breath away. Hold on tight. Hope you enjoy the ride.

By the way, make sure you have your seat belt on.

Peace and love, sincerely,

Frank Marotta

CHAPTER 1

MOMMY DEAREST & OUR DYSFUNCTION JUNCTION

"*You're getting shit for Christmas, all of you Shit, you bitch bastards!*" The year was 1964. President Lyndon Johnson signed the Civil Rights Act into law. Congress authorized war in Vietnam. The Beatles took America by storm. The World's Fair began, launching our Queens neighborhood, Corona, into worldly fame. The United States was thriving. But for me, 1964 was just the beginning of my fragile story of survival.

That Christmas was just like any other; my siblings and I eagerly watched my mother, Rosie, decorate the Christmas tree, hanging on her every moment in hopes she would have a change of heart and let us join in. I now understand that, for Rosie, life raising six kids in a two-bedroom apartment couldn't have been easy. But her Christmas tree torture tactic was just the tip of the iceberg of Ma's complex, confusing, and chaotic personality.

In today's world, where we can openly acknowledge mental-health issues, Ma most likely would have been diagnosed as bipolar. She was also abusive on many levels. We all yearned for just normal love, along with your basic hugs and kisses. We were beaten, though, during her many fits and rages. Over time, she inflicted many physical and emotional scars on us. We could never understand her motives.

To add to her complexities, in the outside world she was a devout Catholic: She never missed a Sunday Mass. She sent us all to Catholic school, where we were abused by the grey nuns of the Sacred Heart. She belonged to the Rosary Society, the Mother's Club, the local Democratic Club. She would work for the New York State Board of Elections. Only her kids knew of her monster side, in that stressful two-bedroom apartment.

My father, on the other hand, was a gentle giant. He was known as *Big Frank*. He was six foot two, two hundred and sixty pounds. He was indeed an imposing figure. When he walked into a room, everyone knew it. He was the quintessential tall, dark, and handsome. He always smelled great, too. He always worked two jobs. We didn't get to see him that much. What we did see though, was his dedication, love, and respect for our mother, in spite of all her craziness and shortcomings. Dad had the patience of a saint.

Dad was a country boy from Schenectady, New York. That would all change in a hurry when he got a taste of a real city slicker, settling into Corona, Queens. Dad and Mom have quite a story as to how they met. My mother's father's brother married my father's father's sister in Italy. Given that scenario, you can say in a way that my mother and father's marriage was actually prearranged.

Dad was very talented. He played many instruments and also had a great voice. He actually played in a country-Western band in his hometown just before him and Ma married back in 1947.

In our house, my grandparents—my mother's parents—lived across the hall. That was also where my mother had lived up until she got married. I spent most of my time at Grandma's. There was no fear across the hall. Grandma gave nothing but unconditional love and comfort. She was my angel. I loved all her stories about the old country. I even learned to speak the dialect my Grandma had spoken in Naples, Italy. My grandfather worked for the Long Island Railroad.

He was a track foreman. His nickname was *Frank the Whip*. He had the record of continued service for many, many years. Fifty-six years, to be exact. Grandpa was very old-school Italian. He had a stern and cold demeanor.

Grandma and Grandpa also had our family's first color television and air-conditioning. So you can see why I never wanted to leave their place. I spent as much time there as I could.

Now, downstairs in our house of gloom lived my mother's younger sister, Josephine. We called her Aunt Jo. She was known as Josie by many. She also had six kids. Needless to say, it was always crazy in our entire house. Between upstairs and downstairs there were a combined twelve kids. Doors slamming, constant noise, always drama. I called it "The Rosie and Josie Show."

It seemed like they always had a baby-making contest. They were always pregnant at the same time. Josie's husband, Uncle Al, was an enigma. He would constantly put my father down and many times disrespected him. Uncle Al also traumatized me as a kid a few times. All that being said, we never did see eye to eye. That was fine with me.

This was also the year I started my baseball career as a Little Leaguer. From an early age, I knew baseball was my passion. The New York Yankees were my team. I will never forget the first time I laid eyes on Yankee Stadium. I felt as if I were floating on air. The clear blue sky, the smell of the beautiful green grass, the smells of the hot dogs, the popcorn, the peanuts. Pure euphoria. Baseball also became my escape, growing up. It gave me solitude from my otherwise pure hell of a childhood. I spent hours just throwing a ball against my house and catching it. Through much practice and dedication, I was able to be talented enough to receive multiple Most Valuable Player awards at an early age. I always played with the older kids. As I loved baseball, baseball had a love for me, the way I always needed to be loved.

"*A prayer for a fare*" is what my father would say to any clergy he met while he was a conductor on the Long Island Railroad. In 1966, our entire family needed all the prayers we could get. The trains at that time had steps that had to be released from the floor in order to extend out so you could exit the train. This particular night, as the train pulled into its last station, Big Frank bent down to release the steps. Unfortunately, the steps did not cooperate. They instead jammed. He had to exert extra force to lift the steps out. As a result, he felt a tremendous pain in his lower back.

When he got back to his office, he informed his supervisor as to what happened. He had to fill out an on-duty injury report. His supervisor wished him well as he punched his time clock and headed home. It was a really tough and long ride. He knew that the outcome would not be good for him and his big family. As he arrived home and just barely made it up the steps to the door, he was in a lot of pain, and bent over. Rosie came to the door and said, "Jesus Christ, what the hell happened to you!?" He told her. He also said he needed to take something for the pain and just wanted to go to bed.

After a rough, uncomfortable night, Dad opened his eyes to the bright morning sun that was trying to make its way through the windows of the bedroom. He wished that the beautiful sunshine of that day would translate into a bright future. In reality, the daylight actually foreshadowed the gloom of things to come. Rosie got up with him and made her first phone call to Dr. Russo, an orthopedist. She told him about Dad and he said to bring him right in. Our neighbor Sal drove them to the doctor.

They did a few tests, and it was determined that Dad dislocated three discs in his lower back. The prognosis was not good. Dr. Russo strongly recommended surgery. The Railroad doctors had an extreme difference in their medical recommendations. The Railroad would only allow Dad to go back to work if he followed *their* protocol. Dr.

Russo strongly disagreed with their proposal, and he did eventually do the surgery. Since the Railroad disapproved, they would not let Dad back to work After seeking legal counsel, Dad commenced a lawsuit. After a long litigation process, Dad won the lawsuit. The win turned out to be a long-term loss. He lost his job, nineteen years of service, and a lifetime pension. We managed a little consolation, Dad bought a brand new Ford Country Squire station wagon. It was the first car we could all fit in as a whole family. Dad's decision to file a lawsuit against the railroad did not sit well with GrandPa Frank. Being that he had held such a high standard working for the LIRR with an exceptional reputation. It would fracture the long term relationship between the two Franks and ultimately add to my Mother's loaded cart of internal frustrations, in the family atmosphere.

    Two years had passed since his injury. It was a real dark moment in time for all of us, but we were now able to reconstruct and begin to see a new shining light. The monumental hardships we faced and the outpouring of love and support from our church and community made us ever so much stronger as a family. It was now time for me to start thinking about moving on. Hopefully leaving dear Mommy Dearest, and that Dysfunction Junction in the rearview mirror.

CHAPTER II

A QUEEN'S CROWN

*G**oodbye to Rosie, the Queen of Corona, seein' me and Julio down by the schoolyard.* Paul Simon was inspired to write these lyrics in his song in his teenage years. He had a fascination with his neighboring community of Corona, Queens, along with all of its characters.

Located in the heart of Queens, New York, it was much more than your typical Italian neighborhood, back then when I was growing up. Unfortunately, its reputation, from the early 1900s, was tarnished. It was the location of one of NYC's landfills. So it was labeled The Corona Dumps.

That all changed in 1939. Corona would have the unique distinction of being the site of the 1939 and then the 1964 World's Fairs.

Over the years, the list of people that were born and raised in Corona, or just grazed its landscape, was very impressive. Jazz great Louis Armstrong lived on the north side of town from the 1940s till he passed away in 1971. His house is now a New York City Landmark and National Museum. It is visited by tourists from all over the world. Another Jazz great Dizzy Gillespie lived just around the block from Armstrong. World-renowned movie man Martin Scorsese, widely regarded as one of the most significant and influential directors in film history, was born in Corona in 1942. From the fashion and cosmetic world, Estée Lauder began her empire from the small kitchen in her Corona apartment. As an inspiring young singer from the state of

Michigan, a music icon settled in Corona as a teenager. Searching for the bright lights of New York City, she formed her first band with locals The Breakfast Club. She went on to achieve worldwide fame and fortune. Her name was Louise Ciccone. You know her as Madonna.

The general consensus in Corona was that it was a great and magical place to grow up. Having the backdrop of the two World's Fairs easily made that statement understandable. It was composed of first, second, and third-generation Italians. People that came into Corona to shop or visit would take notice in an instant of the pride and dedication that their properties had on display. We also had the Lemon Ice King. Voted the best italian ice in New York City many times. It was also a part of the promo for the T.V. sitcom, The King Of Queens.

The year was 1972. It was the Watergate Scandal and the Munich Olympic terrorist attack. The first digital watch was introduced. So was the first handheld calculator. The last of the ground troops were withdrawn from Vietnam. The film *The Godfather* was released. Home Box Office became the first cable service in the USA.

On this particular afternoon, like I always did, I went down to where the mailboxes were located in the front hall. Our front entrance had a distinct exquisite flare. With its polished brass mailbox and its beautiful black and white Italian marble walls, floors, and steps, all visitors or vendors that entered would comment on its impressiveness. The particular piece of mail now in my hand suddenly caught my curious attention.

The return address, in bright red letters said, *Riverfront Stadium, Home of the Cincinnati Reds*. Well, with my shock and amazement, along with my now weakened legs and fluttering heart, I began to read the letter. It said that I have been invited to a tryout camp. *Wow!* I could now bear witness to an actual dream coming true, right before my own eyes.

I hurried up the steps and told everyone. I then hurried down the steps, went outside, and told every friend that could be found. The tryout was to be held in Levittown, Long Island. So Dad and I made it out there on a bright August day. An opportunity of a lifetime for this obsessed baseball kid, indeed. I was one of the youngest players at the camp. I had the absolute thrill of swinging a real Major League Baseball bat and even wore an authentic Reds helmet. I didn't take souvenirs away from that magical day. What I did take was a dream come true. A gratification that would stay with me for a lifetime. How many kids that love the national pastime can honestly say they tried out for a Major League Baseball team?

In Corona, most of our backyards were not big enough to actually play in or otherwise entertain ourselves. They were basically used to do what most Italians did: grow vegetables. All us kids found that the local schoolyard was the place to spread our wings, have fun, and just do what we wanted. After all, there were no parents around there to supervise. The Spaldeen was what we all had. It was an extremely popular small pink ball. It was a must for any and all games.

The schoolyard was our solace from dawn till dusk. It was where our sports heroes came to life. Where you broke in those new sneakers. You would get your first black eye there. Disputes were settled. We even got to learn about the birds and the bees from the more experienced kids.

In Corona, we all had nicknames. I never knew the origin of a lot of them. I guess it really didn't matter. Here are some that stood out and also had the distinction of sticking with their owners well into adulthood: The Rat, The Mouse, The Snake, The Foot, The Peg-Leg, The Ear, The Cow Head, The Bull Head, Porky, Peewee, We-we, Peppy, Blacky, Whitey, and Bucky. By the way, I never was tagged with one. To this day, I never knew if that was a good or bad thing.

Every summer, for two weeks in July, we celebrated The Feast of Our Lady of Mount Carmel. It was very traditional in NYC to see many of these Italian festivals from Manhattan to the Bronx, from Brooklyn to Queens. It was a carnival setting along with traditional Italian food. I can still see the scene vividly and smell those wonderful sausage, peppers, and onions sizzling on those busy oversized grills on those hot summer nights. Many of the locals worked the feast. My parents had a meatball-hero stand. One night, my mother made 600 meatballs. Sold them all.

On my block, we didn't say *street*. The little chapel that housed the statue of Our Lady of Mount Carmel had been built in 1927 by the very hands of the dedicated, hardworking men in this, their beloved neighborhood. I was even an altar boy there. I also had the honor every Sunday morning to ring the bell in the bell tower for the eight thirty mass. I used to think about the Hunchback of Notre Dame.

The only problem with the feast was that the neighborhood guy who would kind of organize and run it didn't have such an acceptable reputation. I'll call him Angelo. The word on the street was that he was stealing money from the proceeds that were supposed to go to the church. This did not sit well with the Corona people. It was time that these low, underhanded, despicable acts by Mr. Angelo were addressed. The old-fashioned way. You see, most Corona guys graduated from the school of hard knocks. So when it came to the subject of retaliation, they were all A-plus students.

So we all put our heads together and came up with a game plan. Since we all lived on the block, we would have complete liberty to execute it. The feast began around five p.m. We had the entire day to work with. It was agreed that a fuse line about twenty-five feet long would be placed under and alongside the tent where Mr. Angelo worked, the gambling tent. On the end of the fuse, there was to be a cherry bomb. When the night got into full swing and Angelo was standing at his normal spot, the fuse would be lit and the explosion of the cherry bomb would commence. This all had to be done precisely and strategically. Ronnie just so happened to live right across from the tent. This made him the leader and mastermind. Ultimately, he would inconspicuously light the fuse.

The stage was set. The drama and suspense was palpable. We were sitting in front of Ronnie's house as his mother brought out a fresh pot of coffee, along with some popular Italian pastries. The feast was now in full swing. We could hear Angelo's loud, obnoxious voice as he announced the winning numbers.

It's nine p.m. Ronnie makes his way to the fuse on the size of the tent. Lights it with a book of matches. Turns around nonchalantly and meets up with us in front of his house. As Ronnie's mother pours us another cup of coffee, *BA BOOM!* The bomb explodes. Right where Angelo was standing. People started to run in all directions. We continue to enjoy those Italian pastries.

It all was a smashing success! Luckily, no one was seriously injured. It was a wake-up call for Angelo, though. The next night, he was telling people that whoever did this would pay a *big* price. Little did he know, he would never find out who was behind the scenes on that hot summer Saturday night.

The summer sunshine of 1972 did certainly end with a *bang!* Ultimately, the cast of characters from Corona got the last laugh—and a little sweet revenge.

Alterations To A Life Jacket

MOM AND DAD'S WEDDING DAY NOVEMBER 22, 1947, CORONA, NY

THIS IS ME AT TWO YEARS OLD. MY MOTHER SAID THAT PEOPLE THOUGHT I WAS A GIRL. DO IN PART TO ALL THOSE GOLDEN CURLS.

ROSIE DECIDED THAT AFTER MY FIRST HAIRCUT, SHE WOULD SAVE THOSE GOLDEN CURL'S. SHE PRESENTED THEM TO ME, MANY YEARS LATER, IN THE ORIGINAL BOX , THAT THEY WERE STORED IN. I STILL TREASURE THEM SOME 65 YEARS LATER.

THIS IS OUR FAMILY AT THE TRAIN STATION IN SCHENECTADY, NY. CIRCA 1962. TOP ROW LEFT TO RIGHT IS ANTHONY, MOM AND DAD, MICHAEL IN FRONT OF ANTHONY, THE TWINS, JOHNNY AND JOEY, IN FRONT OF MOM, ME AND MARY ANNE IN FRONT OF DAD.

Alterations To A Life Jacket

THIS IS MARY ANNE'S FIRST HOLY COMMUNION. ALONG WITH ME AND ANTHONY AT ST. LEO'S CHURCH.

THIS IS ME AND THOMAS WHO SPONSORED ME ON MY CONFIRMATION DAY. THOMAS WAS LIKE ANOTHER SIBLING TO US.

THIS IS MY NEWTOWN HIGH SCHOOL GRADUATION PHOTO.

THIS IS AT MOTHER'S 60TH BIRTHDAY CELEBRATION. SHE INSISTED ON THIS PARTICULAR PICTURE OF HER 5 SONS. SHE USE TO TELL PEOPLE THAT HER FIVE SONS WERE AS DIFFERENT AS THE FIVE FINGERS ON HER HANDS.

THIS IS ME AND THE BEGINNING OF MY BASEBALL CAREER.

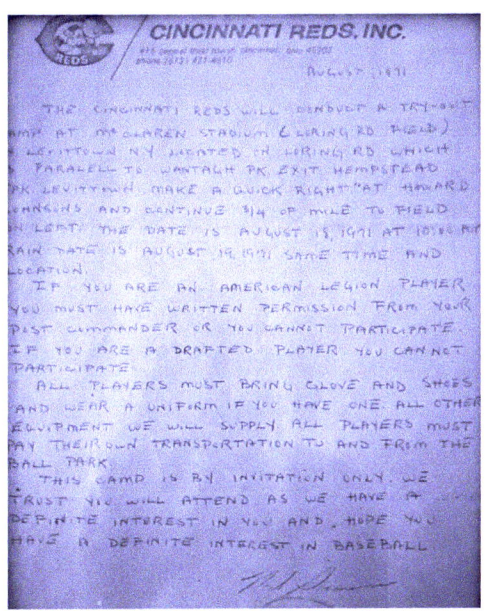

THIS IS THE OFFICIAL TRYOUT LETTER.

Frank Marotta

THIS IS THE ENVELOPE IT CAME IN, INCLUDING THE SCOUTS BUSINESS CARD. ALSO INCLUDED IS A SCOUT'S CARD FROM THE PHILADELPHIA PHILLIES, WHO ALSO SHOWED INTEREST.

CHAPTER III

THE QUEST TO LEAVE THE NEST

The high school that I went to—Newtown High School in Elmhurst, Queens—had a similar distinction to that of my neighborhood, Corona. Some notable alumni: Gene Simmons, Carroll O'Connor, Don Rickles, and, from the world of Major League Baseball, Omar Minaya. In the years I attended, it also had the largest student population in New York City. Over 6,300 students matriculated. In my freshman year, back in 1968, my class was part of history; we saw the first ever NYC teachers strike. Upon graduation, I decided to enroll at the local community college.

I considered myself an average student. Honestly, the education part wasn't really on my mind or radar. Baseball was still my driving force and passion. I figured if I could play college ball, that would be really awesome. It would also allow me to carry on with my eternal dream.

Well, I made the team and was flying high like a kite. Unfortunately, that kite didn't fly too high or too far. I had to drop a class in order to make it to the daily practices, which lowered my GPA. You have to maintain a certain GPA in order to play, and the dropping of that class put mine below the required level. Hence, I was not eligible to play.

I can still vividly remember that terrible, disheartening day in that small smelly men's locker room when Coach Lembo nonchalantly uttered those crucial dream-killing words, "Hey, Marotta, you can't play!" I just sat there on the old soiled wooden bench, shocked and bewildered. I put my hands in my face, and my hands caught my falling tears. That day, any ounce of desire I had to continue my education just left the pores of my skin. The next day, I quit school.

At eighteen, most of my friends were very fortunate to have had cars and girlfriends. Not me. This stemmed, I'm sure, from the wounds of my past, which created so many ill, deep, and suppressed feelings. Two of the most powerful were an extreme low level of self-esteem, basically at empty, and overall self-confidence the size of a grain of white rice.

But since my College days had come to an abrupt end, it was time to ponder another future.

There's a phrase I heard as a kid that has always stuck with me. My father would say it often; so would his friends. It was like a constant neighborhood echo: *In life, it's not what you know, but who you know.* It became a sort of a backdrop to my progressively growing ears—and my life. The older I got, the more it sunk in and the more meaningful it became. *One hand washes the other.*

Those haunting terms and their origin always puzzled me. Was it an Italian thing, or was it a Corona thing? Whatever it was, believe me, it would be a large influence in my life, many, many times . . . always with positive, outstanding results.

It was time now to get a job. I made it my business to circulate my interest to as many contacts as I possibly could.

Well, to my amazement, I didn't have to look or go too far. .My mother, surprisingly, made the first move for me. It was very unexpected. She called a dear friend. Their relationship went way back to the high-school days. We all loved Josephine. She had an infectious laugh. She was extremely funny, and it felt as though my siblings and I had known her for a lifetime. Jo had a nephew who was a big shot for a large supermarket chain. So in about two weeks, I got my first job, thanks to beloved old cheerful Josephine.

The only thing I was not too happy about was it involved working overnights. I had to bite the bullet. Hey, it was a job and a steady paycheck, and I even got into the union. I was able to save some money and buy my first car. It was a 1966 black Chevy Impala. I always knew that my first car would be black. It gave me some freedom, and boy was it a real confidence booster. It wasn't as fancy as the other kids' cars in the neighborhood—as a matter of fact, it was an old man's type of car. It didn't bother me at all. I was an old soul anyway. A match made in heaven. I was moving up in the world.

The job was going pretty well, but for the first time in my life I was up all night and sleeping all day. I could feel my body screaming for some normalcy, but I had no choice. Unfortunately my supermarket career, just like my college career, didn't last as long as I would have liked it to. One night, opening a large box of vegetable oil with a straight razor, I slipped and put a pretty bad gash in my right leg. As I began to feel faint and the blood began to seep through my jeans, I sat there and tried to gather my thoughts.

A coworker came over to help me as the flow of blood continued to the white tiled floor. He got a roll of paper towels. My friend brought me to the Emergency Room, which was not far—and, thank goodness, pretty empty, since it was the middle of the night. The cut required fifteen stitches, plus I had to get a tetanus shot. That hurt like hell.

When I got back to work, I thought I would just fill out an injury report and then head back home. That's what I thought, but my supervisor—a big imposing German guy named Bill—thought differently. He ordered me back to work. I thought that was just inhumane. I told him I was hurting. He basically didn't want to hear it.

Me, naturally being a good guy and nonconfrontational, I returned to my cooking and baking aisle.

But I could not believe that Mr. Bill told me to go back to work. I punched the old, shaky green time clock at the shift's end and headed home. I called in sick the next two nights. On the third night, Mr. Bill saw me and told me to come to his office. I had a gut feeling as to what he was gonna say. He basically said, in an unsympathetic tone, "We have to let you go."

I didn't question his decision, but what I did question was his humanity. I got up, walked out, and left my supermarket career in the past. Every time I see a Mazola oil container, I think of those first fifteen stitches and that empty, brightly lit emergency room. And that lousy tetanus shot.

It was now back to square one. A new job search was at hand. I didn't have a clue where, or what, or *when* a new one would appear. That turned out to be not until I ran into a lifelong Corona friend, Jimmy, whose father had a big job with the New York City Health and Hospitals Corporation. We were just shooting the breeze in a Corona landmark, Spaghetti Park. I didn't know that he was also looking for a job. So he mentioned to his father and said that he would ask him to put out a search for us.

We continued to catch up and we both enjoyed an Italian ice, soaking in the history of the park. When it was time to go, Jimmy said he would call. After about a week, he did call—with some great news. His father could help us out. *Wow*, I thought. *There's that echo again.*

He got me an interview with a local hospital called Elmhurst General for the position of Medical Records Clerk. It sounded somewhat interesting. The hospital was only about fifteen minutes away. I started on April 1, 1974. When I called Jim and told him how grateful and appreciative I was for what his father had done for me, he said his father said it was his pleasure, and that he had always liked me because I was a loyal friend to Jim. That made my day.

So I arrived at the hospital at seven thirty for the eight a.m. start. I made a pit stop at the first floor men's room (which I found would not pass a cleanliness test anytime soon). A medical-records department usually has the reputation of being the armpit of a hospital, I guess because they are often dimly lit and seem to have had the windows open during a passing dust storm. The charts were just busting out all over the dark gray metal racks that they were desperately trying to sit on.

As I entered the department, I was greeted by David Fuller, a well-dressed, sharp-looking Black guy. He was in his early forties. He began to introduce me to the entire staff. It was made up of one other Black guy and a few women who were Hispanic or West Indian. Everyone was very nice and accommodating. When one of the Hispanic women heard my name, she without hesitation said, " Oh boy, my ex-husband's name is Frank." I had no idea what she was implying— and to blurt it out in front of the whole staff, I thought. was kind of weird. *No filter*, I guessed.

What saved her from a weak first impression was what she looked like. Very sharp with her clothes and shoe selections. Hair and makeup, magazine worthy. All the right things in all the right places. The whole package got my undivided attention pretty quick. I figured she was around twenty-five. The fact that she was also quick to tell me, a complete stranger, her marital status also was quite interesting.

The first aisle housed charts starting with numbers 00, and the last aisle started at 99. Her assigned chart aisle was the 70s; mine were the 80s. We struck up a conversation quite easily. Her English, not her first language, was very impressive.

It was now lunchtime. Carmen and I made our way down to the cafeteria. As we were walking through the contrasting green colored halls, I noticed that she was turning quite a few heads. At the lunch table, our conversation began to intensify and flow effortlessly. She said that she had been separated for eight years from her husband and had two daughters. They were nine and ten. I told her she looked pretty young to have kids that age. She was flattered. She told me she was thirty.

She went on to tell me that she came to New York from Puerto Rico when she was fourteen. Her family settled on the Lower East Side of New York City. She also explained to me that she met her husband, also Puerto Rican, at a party when she was eighteen. She continued: that after shortly dating, she became pregnant. In those days with those extenuating circumstances, mariage usually followed. She stated she was nineteen at the time.

I felt that she was dishing a lot of personal information out pretty fast. It really made me wonder. The conversation turned to me. I told her I was nineteen and Italian. I lived in Corona and was one of six kids. She asked if I had a girlfriend. When I told her no, she seemed surprised. She said, "A good-looking guy like you with no girlfriend, I find hard to believe." As a result of our deep conversation level, it became apparent that there was now a mutual comfort zone brewing.

After a very interesting, ice-breaking lunch, we headed back up to work and continued our conversations between aisles 70 and 80. It was indeed a very eventful first day of work, on many counts.

As the days and weeks quickly passed, the chemistry between the Italian and the Puerto Rican grew like an out-of-control fire with wild abandon. We found ourselves sitting on a nearby dark green park bench at lunchtime one day, under a beautiful blue and sunny spring sky with America's pastime in full swing. We gazed into each other's eyes. I took her hand and said, "You may think I'm crazy, but I'm feeling something really special with you." She said, "Well, I guess I'm crazy too!" I tasted her soft, beautiful lips for the very first time and smelled her refreshing, soothing, exciting perfume as we embraced. On April 26, 1974, way ahead of schedule, we had our first date.

CHAPTER IV

YOU MAKE ME FEEL BRAND NEW

In 1974, President Richard Nixon resigned. The Sears Tower became the world's tallest building. *The Exorcist* was the big movie. The first MRI scanner was introduced. On a Saturday morning in Corona, most of us guys would get up at the crack of dawn and start the day by washing and waxing our cars. We would make sure with precise detail and effort that our car would be the best-looking one on the block. It was an unofficial competition.

I had been on the awkward side as a young teen. Being a bonafide jock, my dating career was not at all exciting or, would I say, adventures. My three relationships, if I had to categorize them as such, were bordering on platonic. The only common thread was that all the girls were Italian. To get to first base was doable; second base would be a real stretch. Now it was my time to step up to the proverbial plate with a real woman.

Carmen Carmelita Colon was my ultimate challenge. I honestly did not know what to expect emotionally or mentally. On the other hand, I had a pretty strong hold on the physical part. She lived in Jackson Heights, a neighborhood not too far from Corona. It had a completely different feel from what Corona was all about. It was very commercially loud and noisy and consisted of many apartment buildings that were so close together you could barely fit a toothpick in between them. It had a hustle and bustle to it. Parking was nearly impossible. An elevated subway train was a main fabric of its landscape as it rumbled overhead throughout the day and night.

    I was to pick her up at six p.m. Her sister was going to take the kids till the next day. Carmen's entire family had good wishes for her, as this would be her first ever date since her separation. It was a very special—and long overdue—date for me also.

    My mother, Rosie, took notice of my preparations with a sense of astute curiosity, like the Pope was coming to town. Her big, sharp eyes followed my every move as I prepared for my big night. Now, the very sad part of all of this was that I could not tell her that I was going out with Carmen and all the so called baggage she came with. That would have not gone over very easily. My mother's only comment was, "I hope it's a nice Italian girl!"

    I left my house beaming with hope and pride, feeling and looking sharp, and having made sure I had enough cologne on. I got in my Chevy and headed out to the concrete jungle of Jackson Heights. I reached Carmen's apartment building at precisely six p.m. I was always a proponent of punctuality. I blew the horn two times signaling that I was there. She came down eight minutes later, which I had no problem with.

    She looked absolutely stunning, wearing a red midriff blouse, white bell-bottomed pants, and red high heel shoes, not to mention her perfect hair and makeup. She was a wonderful sight for sore eyes. The first thing she said was, "Wow—I never saw a car so clean and shiny!" That made me feel a real sense of accomplishment; it was exactly what my subconscious needed to hear. The battle plan was dinner and a movie, and what would happen after that was anybody's guess. We stayed local and went to a nice little Italian restaurant in Corona located opposite a pretty tree-lined park in Corona. Ferrara's was a rather small place with a great atmosphere, fantastic food, and soft Italian music. They made it feel like home.

Now, there was actually a little twist and risk in going there. If I saw someone from the neighborhood I knew, and if they knew my parents, it would not be too kosher. Luckily there were no familiar faces—or dagger eyes—to be concerned with.

The conversation was entertaining, educational, and enlightening. Carmen gave me a brief background as to when she and her family settled in the Lower East Side of New York City. She went on to say that it had been a dark and uneasy time. Her family faced tons of discrimination back in the 1950s, as the Puerto Rican people were the first wave of Hispanic immigrants to the United States. She explained that Puerto Rico was a commonwealth of the United States. This actually made them automatic US citizens.

She said she experienced many sleepless nights in those days. A lot of fear, tears, and anxiety not knowing from one day to the next what was going to happen. It was really bad for her and the family. She remained extremely proud of her heritage.

Her brother Pablo joined the army when they came to New York City. Carmen told me that while in a bar one night, in uniform, he was beaten nearly to death by a group of white men, just for being Puerto Rican . My eyes really opened up that night to the plight of the Puerto Rican people, and my empathy for her family grew.

After dinner, and all of that heavy-duty conversation I digested along with my spaghetti and meatballs, we headed out to the movies. Carmen complimented me on my driving skills along the way. I wasn't used to all those nice compliments. We arrived at the Midway theater and took seats in the very back. It was very relaxing, especially after a great Italian meal. My head was still spinning with all I'd just absorbed about her, but it was a good headache. We cuddled tightly and softly kissed in between the buttered popcorn, the napkins and the jumbo Coca-Cola. After the movie, we headed out to my car arm in arm, heart to heart.

Alterations To A Life Jacket

The usual drill after dinner and a movie for us Corona guys was to park in a nice dark, secluded area. We called them Lovers' Lanes. The place I chose was called Jet Park. It was the parking lot on the grounds of the old World's Fair, in front of the Hall of Science, one of the fair buildings that remained. It's still there, and it features replicas of the rocket ships that went into space. They were located not too far from where the car was parked.

It was a dark and peaceful night. Just enough light was peeking in over head from the stree.tAt first we just shared some light conversation. I guess we were both waiting for Mother Nature to kick in. Boy did she kick in, and fast. With those rocket ships in the background, I was ready to blast off myself. "AYEYAIYAI"! Carmen suggested we go back to her place. I couldn't agree more.

We left my home turf and that famous Jet Park and headed to Jackson Heights.. As we reached her block, I anticipated the parking was gonna be rough, but I was wrong. Like someone was watching over and knowing what was about to take place, I got a spot right in front of her building. Divine intervention.

She lived on the second floor in a one-bedroom apartment. When she opened the door, I felt I was entering a sanctuary, a great combination of sensuality and spirituality. There were candles in every direction my eyes could see. The scent of the apartment was captivating. It was as protective as a new piece of clothing.

We continued Mother Nature's commands while our bodies engaged as one on the living-room couch. We redirected to a much more comfortable location: her king-sized bed. As our bodies continued to collide, so did our passion.My long overdue anticipated first sexual encounter became reality. We did not want our mutual bliss to end. But like all good things, it did. We embraced, said our goodbyes and agreed about the joyous night we'd just had. I made my way down to my car and headed back in the wee hours of the morning to Corona.

On that short drive I had nothing but long thoughts racing through my head. Validation, confidence, sexuality, adoration, self-esteem . . . to be able to experience all of that in a twenty-four-hour period was surreal. I hadn't yet been in those places once in my nineteen years of existence. Words cannot accurately describe it all. Like I said, I had only had a few casual relationships in my teens and maybe got as far as second base. That night, I was able gleefully to hit the biggest home run in my life. I could not wait to tell two of my best friends, Anthony and Carl, all about it. It just so happened the next day we were going to the Yankee Game, ironically at Shea Stadium.

CHAPTER V

GOODBYE MACARONI & MEATBALLS, HELLO RICE & BEANS

It was very apparent that we were quickly becoming a hot topic in the dingy world of medical records. I guess our growing chemistry was on display for all to see. I was spending more and more time in Jackson Heights. I could see that it was only a matter of time before I would move in with Carmen.

The other situation that weighed heavily on my mind was that my mother would eventually have to find out about the growing relationship. I had no clue as to how that would play out. I knew quite well that she would have much difficulty in accepting it all. That, you could take to the bank.

I got to meet Carmen's girls shortly after our first date. Myrna was ten and Maria was nine. It was kind of weird to think that I was only nine years older than Myrna. I'm sure she felt the same vibe. As time went on, this and other extenuating factors would rise to the surface and create major problems. For now, it was all new and good and remained a novelty—plus, no one was keeping score.

The girls had contrasting personalities. Myrna was a little standoffish right from the start. Maria was very comical and warm. They were both very athletic. This, of course, sat well with me. When I came into the picture at that time, they saw their Father occasionally. I did not expect the girls to accept me in place of him. I knew it would be a real challenge for all of us. It was uncharted territory for a guy who was just twenty.

Toward the end of 1974 I decided to change my shift at the hospital. This would take us out of the spotlight. Carmen remained on the day shift. Around that time, she encountered a string of health issues that would ultimately lead to her resignation from the hospital. Meanwhile, the child support she was getting from the kids' father was dwindling. At that point, she had no choice but to seek help from public assistance.

She eventually moved to a bigger apartment, just across the street from where she was. I started to meet her family, and they were all very nice and accommodating. She was extremely close to an aunt she spoke very highly of. Aunt Gertie's husband was a NYC police detective. Augie was Italian—and here were myself and Carmen, Italian and Puerto Rican. We hit it off great from the onset. They were warm, welcoming, and extremely generous. We spent a lot of time with them. This was Gertie's second marriage too; her first husband had also been Hispanic.

It happened one day, while passing through Corona with Carmen and the girls. I had stopped for a red light just before the entrance to the Long Island Expressway. A car pulled up on my right and I quickly made eye contact with the driver. It was my dear old Uncle Al. Well, he gave me such a look, which I translated to, "Okay, I have your back against the wall. What are you gonna do now?"

It would turn out to be my worst nightmare. He would now enjoy the pleasure of telling my mother what he'd witnessed at that thirty-second red light.

This was by no means the way I wanted Rosie to find out about my situation. The very next day, Ma said to me, "Sit down." We were in our tiny kitchen, usually a good place to be, but not today. She began to read me the riot act. Her big raging eyes reminded me of those horrific childhood days. *"What the hell is it I hear!? You had an older Spanish woman in your car—with two kids, no less!? What the hell are you thinking!? Are you friggin crazy!? I had a feeling all along that you were lying, you son of a bitch!"*

My world came crashing down like a plane shot out of midair. That was the smallest I have ever felt in my short life. My comeback was explaining that I met her at work, she was a very nice person who was separated with two kids. I told Rosie I felt sorry for Carmen, and I was just trying to help her out. That's all I wanted to tell my mother. Of course, she didn't buy one bit of it. This officially began the long battle I knew I was gonna have to fight. It was all my choice. Nobody had a gun to my head. Still, at only twenty years old, it would not be an easy navigation.

It was now around the summer of 1975. I was thinking very seriously of moving to Jackson Heights, especially now that my mother's and my relationship had taken a turn for the worse.

Shortly after Rosie found out about us, I was about to get another bit of unexpected news, even more explosive than my mother finding out about my relationship. I guess you can call an extension of crucial news. This time, definitely life-altering.

I stopped by Carmen's before going to work. We were sitting in the kitchen having coffee, just a normal chat, when Carmen turned to me and said, "I have to tell you something."

I said, "Okay."

She announced, "I'm pregnant."

I exclaimed, *"What!?"* and she repeated herself. I had hoped that my ears were deceiving me. The sip of hot coffee I had just taken got stuck in my throat en route to my stomach.

"Jesus Christ!" was what I came up with. That wasn't with any religious connotations. It was pure with pure shock, bewilderment, and disenchantment. I suddenly became blind by confusion. Lifeless by numbness. Cold to the touch.

She went on to say that I should not worry. She would take complete responsibility for caring and raising the baby. She said that I was too young for all the responsibility, plus my family would basically disown me. Once I was able to recapture my runaway thoughts, though, my morals, my scruples, my soul, and my DNA came to the forefront.

In those days, the phrase *out of wedlock* carried a tremendous amount of stigma. I didn't want to be ostracized. In order to alleviate it, I suggested we get married. She said it wasn't necessary, but I insisted. Eventually, I was confronted by my parents. Just like what any other parents would say, I heard: *You're much too young for all of that responsibility. How are you gonna feed her and her family? Your life is ruined. You are an embarrassment to our family.* They shredded me to pieces. I told them I would do whatever I had to do to make it work. Looking back, I guess that was my old soul talking. Their final observation was, "You're still crazy."

Before we could get married, there was one major obstacle. Carmen was still legally married. She had to get a divorce—and fast. She found a matrimony/immigration lawyer in Jackson Heights who suggested the Dominican Republic would be the quickest place to get the divorce. She would not need her spouse to sign off on it.

So she left on a Thursday and returned on a Saturday. Her family was gracious enough to pay for the entire trip and the divorce itself. She presented her ex-husband with the divorce papers. He had no issues. At least one early hurdle was accomplished.

On November 5, 1975, we were married in a civil ceremony. Carmen was five months pregnant. I knew my parents and everyone who knew me thought I was crazy. Like they say, love is blind. I guess I was a young man in an old man's shoes. I was determined to give this my best shot. This would indeed be a major stop on the train that would take me on my pretty interesting journey.

CHAPTER VI

A NEW WIFE, A NEW LIFE & HERE COMES THE SON

Being very religious, Carmen made it known that, down the road, she would like to get married in the church, under the watchful eyes of God. It was something that she always dreamed of. I, on the other hand, classified myself more as spiritual than religious. It really didn't matter to me.

Shortly after the holidays in 1975, my sister Mary Anne called me and said she wanted to have a family dinner in our honor. I told her that that would be greatly appreciated. My sister had a heart of gold. About a week later, she and her husband, John, opened their house to the Marotta family. My parents, my siblings with their families, and my godparents, Tommy and Anna, were all there. It would be the first time that my family would meet Carmen and the girls.

You can imagine the anticipation of that night, the physical, emotional, and social challenges that would consume the occasion. You would be able to cut them individually with a knife in the dining room. It would also be adventurous, to be able to feed off everyone's eyes heightening the tone of the room.

By the time we got to the champagne toast given eloquently by my brother-in-law John, I honestly felt the mysterious and unpredictable overall atmosphere lift; things slowly hit a level of normalcy and comfort. At one point, my godfather Tommy, in his frail five-foot-two frame with two yellow fingers on his right hand due to his chain-smoking habit, came over to me and, in a heartfelt tone said, "Frankie, you are now officially a man!" I guess he left the door open for me to read into that.

With the great food and drinks my sister provided, plus some funny Marotta family stories sprinkled in, it turned out to be an excellent time for all. I will never forget what my sister did for us that night. She had no idea that she was setting a positive tone for her brother and his new already-made family amidst an otherwise negative beginning to his new start in life.

I had nothing but optimistic feelings that the new baby's arrival would solidify all good ties with my parents and the immediate family. The pregnancy was coming down the home stretch. Carmen was getting very tired and sluggish. Who could blame her; she gained seventy-five pounds.

Watching my mother control and rule the household all those years, I had a first-row seat on how to do things the Rosie way. We all knew that she was a little nuts. However, her house was immaculate, our shoes were always polished, our clothes spotless, hair perfect. We never went hungry or thirsty, we were always early and never late, no matter where we had to be. It paid off royally for her five sons. We are all domestically educated.

Myrna and Maria were getting very excited about the new baby. The anticipation and drama were building. They actually wanted a baby brother. I told them that I would love a boy too. More importantly, I hoped the baby would be healthy. I had visions and dreams that if I had a boy, he would be my little baseball guy. It had always bothered me that my parents only ever saw me play just once. It made an impression on me forever. I promised myself this would never happen if I were to have a son. Sports and music would be two priorities that I would expose my kids to. There was a very good chance that they would come naturally, since my brothers and I excelled in sports and music was in the Marotta DNA.

I started to bond with the girls pretty quickly. We would often go to parks, have a catch or shoot some baskets. As Carmen got closer and closer to her due date, she became less and less active. This left me with a lot of quality time with the girls. My domestic skills flourished.

On July 4, 1976, the United States celebrated the bicentennial anniversary of the adoption of the Declaration of Independence. "The Spirit of '76" became the backdrop to the year. It went without saying that if you were born that year, you were a Bicentennial Baby. We were extremely lucky and honored to bring our baby into the world during those historical times.

Carmen's due date was March 29th. On Saturday morning, the 27th, her water broke. It was time to get to the hospital—and fast. She was to deliver in Flushing Hospital, the same hospital I was born in. The same hospital where, on September 24, 1959, my mother had delivered the largest twins in the hospital's history: my younger brothers, Joey and Johnny. They weighed 8.3 and 7.11 pounds. Her story was featured in the *New York Daily News*.

On arrival, we went right up to the labor and delivery floor. The delivery went fast and well. At approximately ten thirty a.m., our son came into the world. A big, 9.9-ounce, 23-inch, beautiful baby boy. He was *huge*. With his wide chest and back, he could barely fit in the incubator.

He was born with jaundice due to a high bilirubin count. His skin had a yellow tint to it. To rectify the condition, he had to stay under ultraviolet lights for an extended period of time. This meant that he could not leave the hospital with us upon discharge. He would remain in the neonatal intensive care unit for a week. It was upsetting for all of us.

The first call I made was to my mother. She sounded *so* happy. I told her about his condition. She wished me luck and said she couldn't wait to meet him. Big Frank also got on the phone and also said he couldn't wait to meet him. I was very moved. I then called the girls and they were screaming with joy. I called my siblings and all of Carmen's family. Everyone was so thrilled. I was on the top of the world.

I couldn't believe I have a baby boy. All my own. Naming him was very easy. Frank Marotta, Jr.. I was not my father's junior. To this day, it always bothered me that I wasn't my Father's Junior. He was Frank Anthony. I made damn sure that my son would be my junior. You better believe it.

After a week, Frank Jr. made his grand entrance to the outside world. The girls were ecstatic. Our apartment was on the fourth floor of a walk-up. I had to make a few trips up and down those tough old marble steps that literally took your breath away—not in a good way.

I knew it would take Carmen a while to recuperate from the birth of this big little guy. I jumped in and did whatever had to be done to make this transition for our family go as smoothly as possible.

They say a new baby changes your life forever. Boy are they right. Like in a successful MLB team, or any team for that matter, a good combination of rookies and veterans is always the key ingredient to success. With me being the rookie and my wife the seasoned veteran, we were destined to become a successful winning team.

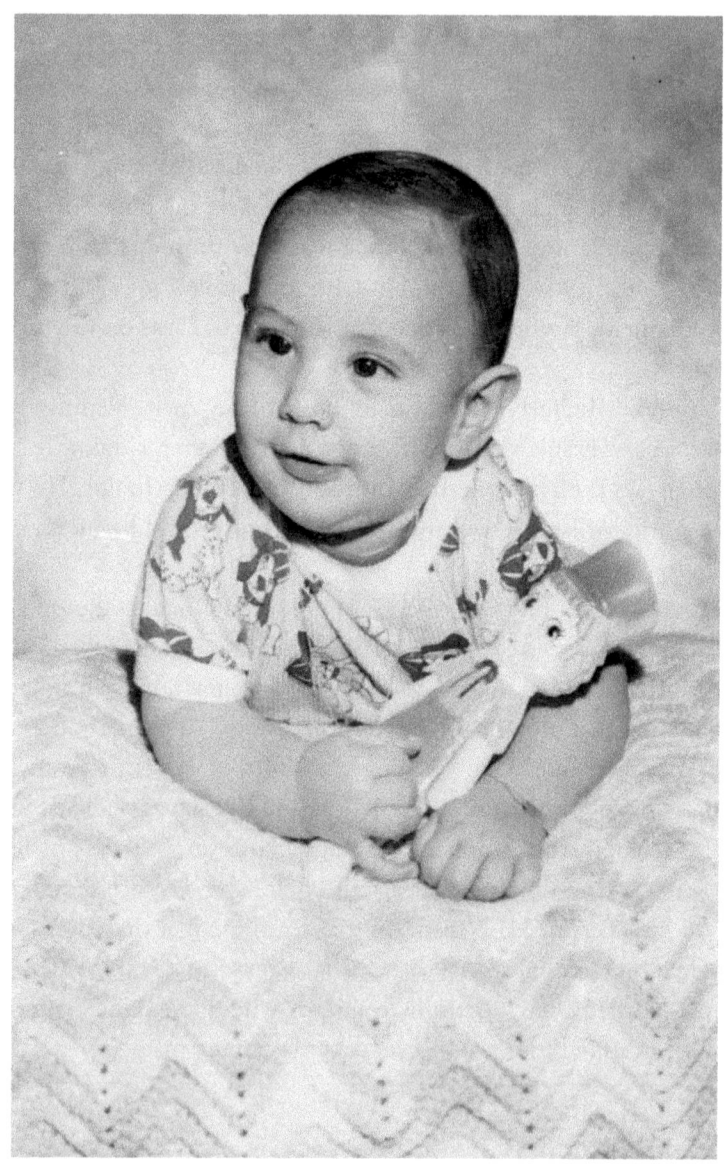

FRANKIE JR. AT 6 MONTHS.

Alterations To A Life Jacket

FRANKIE AND ME IN FRONT OF GRAMMY'S HOUSE.

FRANKIE AT HIS FIRST BIRTHDAY PARTY LOVING
GRANDMA ROSIE'S FAMOUS CREAM PUFFS.

THE ONLY KNOWN PICTURE OF THE 3 GENERATIONS OF FRANKS.

FRANKIE'S FIRST GRADE PICTURE.

FRANKIE WITH HIS FIRST GUITAR.

ME AND MY FIRST CAR 1966 CHEVY IMPALA. BLACK WITH A RED INTERIOR.

CHAPTER VII

THE NIGHTS THE LIGHTS WENT OUT IN THE BIG APPLE

1977 was a crazy and significant year in New York City. On the night of July 13, at 8:37 p.m., the entire city went dark. It was total mayhem: 4,500 looters were arrested, twenty-five mass fires were simultaneously reported; 550 New York City policemen were injured. Mayor Abe Beame reported the following: *This blackout has threatened our health, safety and economy. This never before seen terror and the cost of all its devastation will forever live on, in the hearts and minds of our beloved citizens of this great city.*

The other notable event was the reign of the notorious Son Of Sam. David Berkowitz grew up in New York City and served in the US Army. Using a .44-caliber bulldog revolver, he killed six people and wounded seven. His prime target were teenage girls with long brunette hair. As the number of victims increased, he eluded the biggest police manhunt in the history of the NYPD. The killing spree terrorized New Yorkers and went on to garner worldwide notoriety.

On the night of August 10, 1977, Berkowitz was finally captured by the great efforts of the detective squads of NYC. He was taken into custody and subsequently indicted. In his sworn statement, he claimed to have been taking orders from a demon, manifested in the form of a dog. Berkowitz pleaded guilty to all charges. Since his arrest, he has been incarcerated and is currently serving six consecutive life sentences in a NYS correctional facility.

August 16, 1977 brought the tragic loss of the one and only king of rock 'n' roll, Elvis Presley.

Back on the home front, though, we all were soaking in the complete joy, elation, and happiness brought by little Frankie. Wherever we took him, he was the center of attention, always, with his beautiful brown curly hair and a big contagious smile. His look and spirit was such that people often took him for older than he was.

He was the first grandson on the Marotta side. My older brother Anthony's daughter Lorie had been the very first grandchild. She was born in 1975 and had big blue eyes and beautiful blond hair. We always tried to get the grandkids together, especially in Corona. My grandparents and parents just loved them to pieces.

Frankie's development was quite impressive. He took his first steps at eight months and potty-trained at thirteen. Just around that time, he began to put words together. What got me was the fact that after the traditional first words—*Mommy*, *Daddy*—his next word was *Helicopter*. You would think a kid's few first words would contain one syllable: car, ball, truck, plane. Not Junior. He was just on another platform.

The first time my and Carmen's two families officially met was at Frankie's first birthday party. I got to realize pretty fast how party-oriented the Latinos were. Don't ask me how we fit everyone into our rather small two-bedroom apartment. We needed one room just for the food! Everyone cooked and brought stuff. Now, between the Italians and the Puerto Ricans, you could not find a better combination of any two cultures. The apartment was dominated with two distinct food aromas, and it was both delicious and therapeutic. It attracted our neighbors, who lingered in the hall with curiosity.

We were so happy to have my father's three sisters come all the way from Upstate—Schenectady, New York—to be with us. Growing up, Schenectady had been our summer home. We spent all of our summers there. That's where all our Marotta cousins were, so Kay, Fran, and Jen—plus my grandparents on that side—always made their homes our homes those memorable summers. We just loved the country, even though it was a far cry from Corona.

The highlight of the party was when my father sat down at the piano and started to play. Before you knew it, my three aunts joined in. They sang some standards and country songs. It was *fantastic*. They put on some show.

It reminded me of being upstate. After a traditional Italian Sunday dinner, we all used to gather around my father as he played his accordion. It was just great. We all loved and cherished those special family moments. It was now relieved at my place, and it was just precious. My only regret of those wonderful moments was not taking a video of my pop and his sisters that day, March 27, 1977.

Frankie was sixteen months old and thriving, when one morning that July he woke up with a 102-degree fever. We brought him to his pediatrician Dr. Stein, who was pretty close by, in Astoria, Queens. He told us Frankie had an ear infection, prescribed an antibiotic, and said to keep him in an air-conditioned room as much as possible. The weather forecast was calling for temperatures close to 100 degrees. We did exactly what the doctor told us.

That night he went to sleep at his normal time, around eight p.m. His fever had subsided a bit during the day. And then the power and lights went out.

I got my large favorite red flashlight out. Carmen lit all her religious candles and they flickered all around the house. It was like being in a church, waiting for mass to begin.

To add to our frustration, the batteries in our transistor radio must have been dead. We were clueless as to the reason for the blackout—or how long it would last. We opened all the windows in the apartment. It was gonna be a rough night.

At about ten o'clock, Carmen heard the baby making some noise. No sooner after checking on him did she call me from his room in a frantic tone. I went in, and she said, "The baby feels very hot." So she took his temperature and said, "Oh, dear Lord." His temperature was 106.7.

She picked him up from the crib, I got my flashlight, and down we went. My car was two blocks away. It didn't help in pitch black that the car was also black. "Let me have him," I said, running much faster than Carmen was trying to. We got to the passenger's-side door; I already had my keys out. I opened the door to let her sit first so I could give her the baby. In that instant, to our horror, the baby started to go into convulsions. He was also foaming at the mouth. We were terrified.

Elmhurst Hospital was only three blocks away. I had to be doing forty miles an hour down those three blocks. My heart was racing. I had to get him there in a hurry. That was all I was focused on. I pulled up on the circular ramp leading to the emergency-room entrance, took him from his mother, and ran directly in. This was life-and-death. I began to scream for help, and I laid him down on the first stretcher I saw. A nurse came over quickly and gave him an injection in his right thigh. She told me it was fifty milligrams of phenobarbital, which would control any further convulsions.

The staff was very responsive and professional, and my medical instincts were in high gear. The attending doctor told us that they would need to do a spinal tap in order to rule out spinal meningitis. Due to the high risk of the procedure, they would need signed consent from us.

At that point, the nurse took the baby, and we followed her to a special-procedure room one flight up. They were going to contact the resident doctor on call to do the procedure. Frankie was very groggy and going in and out of sleep. Carm went into the room with the nurse as I stayed out to wait. It was now past midnight.

I was pacing back and forth, very nervous knowing that a six-inch needle was about to enter my little baby's spine. I was on one end of a long, dimly lit hallway. There was an eerie, palpable silence. I worked in a hospital, and I was well aware of the different situations that required certain protocols. There was no sign of life in that hallway.

All of a sudden, I finally saw a person from afar. I couldn't make out anything about them. As the figure got closer, out of the shadows, I saw a man in a lab coat approaching rather slowly with no urgency. *This has gotta be the resident.* He started to rub his eyes and made a sound that resembled a yawn. Now, medically, I put two and two together. This resident was most likely coming off of a very long shift. On top of that, he had been awakened by the emergency-room staff to do the procedure.

There was no way in hell this guy was gonna stick a six-inch needle into my baby's spine. He extended his hand out and said he was Dr. Patel. I came so close to saying, "Why don't you go back to sleep?" Before he could get into the room, I summoned Carm and told her we were not doing the procedure. She looked at me as though I were crazy, and I told her I'd explain later. To the strikingly baffled nurse, I said, "We have to go back to the emergency room. There will be no procedure."

The charge nurse vehemently questioned my decision. I told her I had my reasons and did not go any further. She said "Mr. Marotta, it is very dangerous to take your baby out of here," and told me I would have to sign an AGAINST MEDICAL ADVICE DISCHARGE STATEMENT. I knew exactly what that meant. It would relieve the Hospital of any liability. I told them I was bringing the baby to Flushing Hospital. They put him in cold blankets and off we went.

    Carmen questioned my decision too. I told her that the Resident had been woken out of a dead sleep. "Would you like him to stick a needle in *your* spine?" I asked. There was silence. I guess she got my drift. Flushing Hospital was expecting us, and I was very confident about my decision.

    We went up to the special-procedure room as soon as we got to the hospital. We gave the baby to a nurse and she instructed us to sit in the waiting room. It was only about a half hour that we waited. Then we heard the blood-curdling screams coming from that room of horror. We both broke down and cried. It was torture, to hear your own flesh and blood endure such pain. To this day, I can still hear those horrific screams in my mind like a recurring nightmare.

    We were eventually let into the room. Frankie cried when he saw us. At least they were tears of joy. It was almost time for the sun to rise as we made our way home. It had to have been the most mentally and physically draining day of my life. We got the results of the procedure by phone about a week later. Everything was normal, but the baby had to be on phenobarbital for the next two years. It is a pretty rough deal for a baby to be on a barbiturate. He was a trooper, those two years. It hurt us just as much to be giving it to him. We were extremely lucky on that crazy blackout night. Things could have gone much worse. We were thankful.

CHAPTER VIII

FAREWELL TO OUR GENTLE GIANT

Since I was working the night shift at the hospital, I would on occasion come home on my dinner break from six to seven p.m. One Sunday around five p.m., Carmelita called me at work, to say that my mother had called the house. My mother told her that my father was not feeling well.

Now, my father was like an ox. He was never sick, and I don't ever remember him missing a day of work. Now, something was not sitting right in my gut. Why didn't my mother call me at work to fill me in? Had Dad stayed home? My brain was now in overdrive. I did not like what I was hearing at all. The thought *This can't be good* circled around in my head.

Given the picture my mother was painting, Carm suggested that we go visit Big Frank on my dinner break. I thought that it wasn't a good idea, since I only had an hour. She insisted that we go. I finally agreed. I mentioned to my supervisor that I may be a little late. Being in the habit of disappearing to his car and forgetting about his troubles for a while with his friend Johnny Walker, he couldn't care less. I made the five-minute trip home, having asked Carm to meet me downstairs with Frankie and be ready to go.

Every time we got to the house in Corona, my father would be in his favorite spot, the recliner. The only bad thing about his favorite spot was that it always looked like there was a fire going on under the chair; the smoke all around him resembled a gray cloud, and he was in the middle of it. You see, the vice my father had was smoking. He would start with his L&M cigarette, followed by a big Cuban cigar, followed by his famous pipe with Sugar Barrel tobacco.

Usually, Frankie would run up to him. Dad would catch him and throw him up in the air. When Frankie ran to him that night, though, Dad was not able to pick him up. Dad's normal skin tone was a beautiful olive, but this night it was ashy. Again, all signs leaned south. I was officially upset and concerned. I wasn't planning on telling anyone that, either.

I made my way to the kitchen, which still held the residual breathtaking smell of the Sunday-afternoon meal. I needed to speak to Rosie. I quickly interrogated her under the same bright fluorescent kitchen lights that I'd watched as a kid. She told me that when Dad came home the previous night, he had been extremely upset.

Dad was a doorman in the most luxurious apartment building in Queens, the Kennedy House. The residents were some of the most rich and famous people in the city. They all had one thing in common: They absolutely loved and adored Big Frank. He was their hero.

The night before, as Mom explained, one of Dad's good friends, a dentist, had come into the building through the huge brass revolving doors. He greeted Dad as usual and made his way up to his apartment. About half an hour later, Dad—at his podium in the lobby, looking at the daily newspaper and perusing the Belmont Race Track results—heard an unusually loud and suspicious noise a little way out from the large revolving doors.

He made his way outside and witnessed something that resembled a scene from a horrible, gory, bloody scary movie. After he was physically sick to his stomach, he realized what he was looking at. Scattered body parts in all directions that belonged to his good friend, the dentist. He had decided to end his life by jumping from his blue-lit terrace on the twenty-seventh floor.

To add insult to injury, my brother-in-law John had recently decided to leave my sister Mary Anne. It was a shock to us all. He blindsided her. She was devastated. Dad was hit the hardest. To have to see his beautiful red-headed daughter go through it all played heavy on his already weak heart.

Even though he was built like an ox, Dad did have underlying health issues. He was overweight, had high blood pressure, and suffered from vertigo. They didn't have cholesterol numbers in those days, but if they had, his numbers would have been off the charts. You could also sprinkle in some stress, to that recipe. That Sunday morning after breakfast, he put a major scare into Ma. He briefly fainted and, luckily, fell into his favorite spot. Ma immediately called Dr. Boccia, who had been the family doctor for twenty-five years. He arrived promptly (house calls being common back then), took Dad's vitals, and determined them to be normal. He suggested that he see him again at Parsons Hospital the next morning for a complete workup.

We were ready and about to leave. I held Frankie up so Dad could kiss him. We said our goodbyes to my mother and grandmother. Rosie asked if I could take Daddy to the hospital in the morning. I said of course. I then turned to my father, extended my hand, and received a very strange weak handshake. My father's handshakes were lethal. My very last words that I would ever say to my dear father were, "You better cut all that smoking shit out!"

The next morning, Monday, October 3, 1977, I got up early to be at the hospital by ten a.m.. As I got out of the shower, the phone rang. Carmen answered it. I vaguely heard her say, "Hi, Grandma," and with that, she gave me the phone cause she didn't quite understand what she was trying to say. I guess because Grandma had a heavy accent. "What's the matter, Gram?" I asked. "Hurry up, hurry up—your father is on the floor!" she replied. I was consumed like ash from an erupting volcano. My existence stood silent, frigid, and lonely.

I got dressed in a flash, ran down those annoying four flights of steps, and made my way out to my car. It was two blocks away. I realized that Grandma had called at about 9:25 a.m., and the appointment was at ten. I was driving as fast as I could; my heart was keeping the same pace. I made it there in fifteen minutes. I went up the block, like I have done a million times, but this time like it was my last lap of a major race-car competition. As I pulled in front of 103-46 52nd Avenue, I noticed a police car and an ambulance. Those visions just compounded my inner hysteria along with bringing a false sense of hope. I ran up my childhood steps, by this time with depleted oxygen.

At the top of the landing was a cop in full uniform who looked like he was on a special protective mission or detail. We made eye contact while he took out his handkerchief and cleared his teary eyes. I entered the apartment. The door hung open, and there was a deafening silence. The goosebumps on my arms were quickly multiplying.

In the foyer there had always been a large green refrigerator. It seemed to be slightly moved to the right. To the left of the refrigerator was the bathroom. As I looked down at the floor, I saw what were clearly my father's legs. There he was, lifeless, laying on the bathroom floor. He had taken his last breath at 9:35. Twenty-five minutes away from his ten o' clock hospital appointment. He was only fifty years old.

He had just gotten out of the shower. He wore clean white boxer shorts along with his white round-neck cotton undershirt and a new pair of black nylon socks. Clean-shaven, hair combed, and teeth brushed, along with a good amount of Johnson & Johnson baby powder on his neck, shoulders, and broad back. It was like a vision: he was getting ready for his trip to the pearly gates.

In the kitchen was a lifelong friend, Bob Guida, who owned Guida's Funeral Home in Corona. It was where most of the neighborhood people made their last stop. We hugged and exchanged tears as well. I asked him where my mother was. She is in the living room, he said. Ma was sitting on the couch. As we embraced, the air was cold and numbing. The reality of it all was not registering. The mood was one of pure bewilderment. Ma's eyes remained in a locked position as she desperately tried to make sense of it all.

We found out later on that Dad had suffered a coronary thrombosis. A blood clot inside a major blood vessel in his heart caused the massive heart attack. "*Oh no!*", Ma said, would be his last words.

I was the first of the offspring to arrive. My five siblings arrived in stages after. The youngest, Johnny, unfortunately got there when they were taking Dad down the steps, in a body bag. He had come from the farthest away, as he was driving a truck in Manhattan. My sister Mary Anne was also working in the city. Unfortunately, she also had to see Dad being carried out by the undertaker.

The grieving process was a very arduous one. It was a real rough three days of mourning at Guida's Funeral Home. The outpouring of love, support, and affection was a beacon of light. There were literally lines and lines of people—day and night—paying their last respects to Big Frank.

There are some people in our lives whose impact is so immediate and permanent, it's all but impossible to remember a time when they were ever far from us.

To our dad, our hero, our inspiration, you are forever loved and missed. It's so very true: the good indeed die young. May he rest in eternal peace.

CHAPTER IX

A DETECTIVE & THE BREAKDOWN AT EXIT 17

My mother wore a lot of hats in her day. The *widow* hat was one she never thought she would have to wear at this stage of her life. All the kids but one, Joey, were gone and had made lives of their own. I, Anthony, Mary Anne, and Johnny all got married in our early twenties.. Michael went on to pursue his dreams of one day being on Broadway. He ultimately moved to Manhattan. Joey was your ultimate bachelor. He had a great job with American Airlines. Traveled the world, always had a nice car—and many different women to match. He took Mom on many vacations. The most famous was Italy. Joey stayed home till he was thirty. Eventually, he moved to New Jersey. The sad part about his life was that he battled drug and alcohol addiction for many, many years. He had a heart of gold, but his demons would win in the end. He left us at the young age of fifty-five.

Rosie had no choice but to step up to the plate. She was determined. She even got her driver's license. We had no doubt that she would succeed. She got a job as an assistant librarian for the New York Life Insurance company in Manhattan. She would now be a commuter on the NYC subway, a place she hadn't navigated since her high-school days some forty years earlier. She went on to work fifteen years, received a pension, and never looked back. She was indeed an inspiration to us all. From the mother we saw in our childhood to the mother and proud grandmother she became was truly an amazing transformation.

In 1978, the first "test-tube baby" was born. The first mobile phone made its debut. *Saturday Night Fever* was a big movie. Serial killer Ted Bundy was finally captured for good. My beloved New York Yankees were the world champions.

Little Frankie was progressing at a rapid pace. He was talking like crazy. He had to have had the vocabulary of a four-year-old. He would patiently wait by the front door at midnight for me to come home from work. He loved to sit on the couch next to me and watch *The Tonight Show* with Johnny Carson. He was fascinated—especially with all the singing and musical acts.

Carm and I decided to have another child. We figured that it would be our last. To have a girl would be a special complement to our little boy. Before we knew it, she was pregnant. Her due date was October 16, 1978. She had a rough pregnancy this time around. She really couldn't do much. As usual, I had no problem picking up the slack.

The summer of that year, I spoke to my favorite aunt, Jen. She was my Father's youngest remaining sister in Schenectady. I told her I was thinking of making a trip up with the girls and Frankie. I said that Carmelita was not up to it. I figured we'd come for a weekend. She said, "Absolutely!" So it was a plan. We were to leave early on a Friday and return back early Sunday night.

We left at nine a.m. It was a three-hour ride from Jackson Heights on a bright, beautiful, blue-sky morning. On the drive, I told the kids that when I was little, and even into my early teenage years, my siblings and I would spend most of the summers in Schenectady. I told them how much we loved all of our cousins and that just being in the country was a very special time for us. I told them that Aunt Jen had a big, beautiful house with a tremendous backyard. It had a swing set, a basketball court, and a great big swimming pool. They were amazed and could not wait to get there. Frankie kept on saying, "Are we there yet, Daddy?"

I told them about Aunt Jen's three boys, Donny, Dean, and David, whom they would meet. The anticipation was killing them. This was definitely a highlight in the girls' life, meeting my extended family and being in the country for the first time. You could see the excitement in their eyes.

When we got out of the New York State Thruway at Exit 25 and stopped at the tollbooth, I told them to open up the windows all the way and just smell the fresh country air. I told them that we used to do the same thing all those years past. We finally pulled into the long dirt driveway at about a quarter after twelve that afternoon.

Aunt Jen and the boys heard the car and came out from the back porch. We all hugged and kissed and just took in the special moment. I had flashbacks of days gone by. The kids didn't know what to do first. This was a park at their disposal. The weather was absolutely beautiful all three days. The kids were in their glory. Their body language said it all. We had cookouts and enjoyed Aunt Jen's fabulous cooking. Her Italian Sunday-afternoon meal was to die for. I can still smell and taste her fantastic food.

Like all good times and all good things, they had to come to an end. It was obvious that the kids didn't want it all to end. It certainly was a weekend for a lifetime. Their faces said it all. I figured we would leave before it got dark. It was always what my father would say, back in the day, adding that it was much more dangerous if your car were to break down on a trip while traveling at night. *Make sure you always have a full tank of gas, too*, he would say. We said our goodbyes. You could see that the kids were sad. I thanked Aunt Jen for just a fabulous weekend. We embraced and cried at the same time. Again, flashbacks to all of our emotional departures from Schenectady to head back home to Corona. Aunt Jen added with sincere enthusiasm and graciousness, "Please come back real soon! Please come again!"

Aunt Jen was always my favorite aunt. She is a beautiful person both in and out. She exemplifies pure and genuine love—constantly. I'm proud and honored to still have her in my life

I stopped at the corner gas station, filled my tank, and anticipated a smooth ride home, back to the concrete jungle. It was now 6:15. Most of the trip would have daylight. I figured we should be home by 9:15, according to plan. That was all contingent upon a trouble-free trip. It was wishful thinking, on my part.

Dusk was quickly approaching. The traffic was light. I was averaging around seventy miles per hour. The girls were just taking in the sights, before the darkness. I could, in my rearview mirror, see that Frankie was beginning to fall asleep. My thoughts were consumed by the memories of all those adventurous return trips back home to Corona from Schenectady. Now it was my family, and my time to carry on this tradition.

We were approaching Exit 17—this would mean we were in and around Newburgh, New York (after all those trips, I got to memorize the exits)—when I began to feel that the car was not running right. Then, the gas pedal was not responding to my foot. I noticed, also, that my speedometer was rapidly decreasing. My gas-tank needle was descending to empty. I began to anticipate something that would be out of my control. My senses were at a high level of complete observation.

I made it to the right lane and put my emergency flashers on. The condition became continually worse. I was just about to enter panic mode. As I pulled onto the right shoulder the car just died. Now the night was completely black; just as well were my prevailing thoughts. The girls were visibly frightened, asking "What happened?" I really didn't have a definitive answer. I told them there was a problem with the car. The first thing I was taught as a young driver was when you break down, put your emergency flashers on and lift the car's hood. The only clue I could surmise was that there was a strong smell of gas. I had no choice but to stay calm, given the unexpected circumstance in which I was in. I didn't want the kids to see any other demeanor.

Now, I had seventeen dollars in my pocket—no credit card, and nothing else but lint. I had to get innovative and fast. Like an angel from heaven, a dusty, dirty old red pickup truck, with muddy tires, a cracked windshield, and most likely an exuberant amount of mileage on its engine and transmission, pulled up in front of me. A rather large heavyset man, with a crumpled black baseball hat on his head, distinct roadmap lines on his face, and an unfiltered cigarette dangling from his cracked lips—along with crusty denim overalls, and work boots that were screaming for an upgrade—exited the truck. He approached, and in a heavy Upstate accent said "Howdy! What seems to be the problem, young man?" All I could say was that the car had just died.

He began to remind me that I was in a very dangerous location. He recommended that I be towed ASAP. He offered to reach out to the state police; he had a CB radio in his truck. So that's what he did. He said the police in the area were very good and they should arrive shortly. I thanked him very much and appreciated his concern and his humanity for fellow man. He wished me luck and drove away into the black night heading due south. Even though that guy by no means resembled what a saint looks like, he sure as hell acted like one.

Sure enough, within ten minutes a state trooper arrived, along with his classic gray highway-patrol cowboy hat, pants that looked like they were just pressed at the local cleaners, and a stern, dry, professional, demeanor. He pulled up behind me with his red lights flashing aggressively. He asked where I was headed and what was wrong with the car. I filled him in. He said he would dispatch a tow truck right away. I told him that we had no place to stay the night. He said that there was a Holiday Inn across the street from where the tow truck would bring the car. He suggested I tell them my emergency situation and assured me that they would accommodate me and the kids. He wished me well and headed south on the Thruway.

Now, my homework and absolute dilemma was how the hell in God's name was I supposed to pay for all the expenses I was about to incur. I knew my family: right off the bat, they would have no answers. The relatives in Schenectady might have been an option. At that time of the night, though, the country people that they were, they'd be in their beds for the night. So that option was out. As I waited for the tow truck, I looked up to the dark, star-bright country sky, asking for help and screaming, subconsciously, for answers, hoping for a solution.

Bingo! It hit me like a ton of falling bricks and a piercing lightning bolt. A person that works with emergencies, with life-and-death situations, on a daily basis. The husband of Carm's beloved aunt, New York City Detective First Class, August Peano. A wave of utter relief consumed me. Now I just had to get a hold of him.

In the meantime, the tow-truck driver came, hooked the car up, and told me that there was a gas station downtown in Newburg. I took Frankie, who was sound asleep, and the girls, who were also on the verge of falling asleep, and we all squeezed into the front bench seat of the old and dirty tow truck.

I told the operator my situation and asked him to take us to the Holiday Inn. He was very nice and said it was no problem at all. He dropped the car first at the station and then drove to the hotel.

I gave him my last seventeen dollars and told him that's all I had. He gave me the business card to the gas station and said to call them in the morning as he wished me luck.

So now it was around midnight. I entered the hotel lobby, gave the sleeping Frankie to Myrna, and told them to sit on the lobby couch and wait for me. I headed up to the counter to speak to the hotel clerk. I tell him my dire emergency. He was very understanding and empathetic. I ask to use the hotel phone. He said, go right ahead. My first call was to Carmen. She was very nervous that she hadn't heard from us. I told her what had happened. She said, "Dear Lord, is everyone okay?" I assured her that we were just drained and very tired. I told her we were safe and in a hotel in Newburgh. She said that she would pray for us and ask God to watch over us. I asked her to give me Gertie and Augie's phone number. She did, and I said we'd see her tomorrow some time.

I called and Gertie answered. I knew they usually stayed up late. She asked, "Is everything okay?" and I said, "Not really." I told her the whole story and asked if I could speak to Augie. She said of course, and put him on the phone. So I told him what was going on. I said I had no money and didn't know what to do.

"Here is what we do," he confidently replied. When you know how much the car will be, and the hotel with other expenses, you let me know. I will wire you the money to Western Union in downtown Newburgh."

I thanked the clerk for my use of the shiny black phone. He gave me a key and we headed up to Room 103. After I spoke to Augie, I felt like the world had just lifted off my shoulders. But I still had to execute what he had told me to have everything go smoothly. I hardly slept that night, just thinking of it all. I got up around six and jumped in the shower. When the girls and Frankie got up, they also took showers—the bummer was, we had to put the same clothes back on. At that point, who really cared. We had bigger fish to fry.

We headed back down to the lobby. The kids again waited for me on the large blue couch. I asked the clerk if I could use the phone.

I called the gas station and the guy said that they had to replace the fuel pump. He gave me the price and said it would be ready shortly. I asked the clerk what the fee was for the night. I called Augie back and told him how much I would need.

He said, "No problem. I will wire the money. It should be there in a half hour." I told him that he was a lifesaver and I could not thank him enough. He said, "We are family, and that's what families do."

I will never ever forget what he did for me and the kids that horrible summer night. He was, and still is, a very special human being.

I asked the clerk if he could get me a taxi; he said it would be there in five minutes. I thanked him for his kindness and hospitality. When the driver came, I told him we also needed to go to pick up my car. All went well; I paid the gas station, the cab, and the hotel. Close to the hotel was a diner. We had a great big, warm, satisfying breakfast, and I got my full tank of gas. We could not wait to be home sweet home.

That trip goes down forever in my life's short history. I learned a lot from that experience. It was a true test of my character, courage, fortitude, and wisdom. I would be put to the test on my journey much more than a few times, but not again to that magnitude. So I thought.

CHAPTER X

NO STOMACH FOR THE WORLD OF THE BULLS & THE BEARS

Just prior to the summer of '78, Carmen had gotten a phone call from someone she hadn't heard from in years. It was a long-lost, distant relative's daughter. Her name was Mary. Ever since Mary's mother passed, there hadn't been any communication. When Mary called, out of the blue the relationship was rekindled.

Although she wasn't, really, Carm always referred to Mary as her niece; you can imagine all the catching up they had to do. Mary was now in her late thirties and had just moved back to New York after living in California. She had no idea that Aunt Carmen remarried and had a new baby.

So a visit to Jackson Heights was in order for Mary. I suggested it be a Sunday; I would make a classic Italian meal for us all. It all happened in a matter of two weeks. It was like a family reunion. Mary was very attractive and educated, and there was a great enthusiasm about her. She had beautiful, black, long silky hair, an infectious smile, and a warm and caring personality. She told us how she missed her hometown, New York City. Especially, she points out, the pizza and the bagels.

She had a very close friend in New York who worked on Wall Street. This was the primary reason she came back. Her friend

Barbara had good connections and was able to get Mary a really good job. The company was Merrill Lynch, Pierce, Fenner & Smith. I asked Mary if she could handle the hurricanelike pace of Wall Street and all of its frantic craziness. She said she could handle it.

The conversation inevitably shifted towards me after our three-course dinner as a fresh pot of coffee was brewing. We awaited a dessert of Carmen's classic Puerto Rican rice pudding and of course my assortment of Italian pastries from Corona, which no one could ever refuse. I told Mary that I was working nights in our local hospital in the Medical Records department. She then asked if I liked it. I told her that it was just a job for now and that I could see that it would not be my future, even though I had aspirations of becoming a medical professional . . . one day.

She then asked me if I would be interested in working on Wall Street. I said "Wow, I never gave it any thought." I was kinda taken off guard a bit. I was pretty set in my ways, which, I admit, was not such a good attitude for someone my age. Then again, remember, I walked around with that *old soul* label. I wished, though, that I was more of an optimist. Spontaneous and adventurous would be a nice change of pace. For some reason, this new idea just happened to hit me in a good spot and at a good time. I told her I was interested. She would speak to her boss first thing Monday morning and call me.

I found it difficult to fall asleep that night, thinking about all the different scenarios possible if I decided to make a career move. I knew I would wake in the morning to some curious happenings. That Monday morning at precisely eleven a.m., the phone rang. It was Mary. She said, "I have some great news; my boss wants to meet you."

Wow. He said he would like to see me the following Monday in his office at nine a.m. I told her that would work, and she said she would send me the application in the meantime.

That next Monday morning, I got up real early for my big interview. Got my best suit and tie on along with my new black shoes—and of course my signature cologne. I said goodbye to Carm, she wished me luck, and I was on my way to the Big Apple.

The number 7 train was literally on my corner. It was a baseball throw away. You could hear the constant rumbling of the train at all hours of the day and night. You could have a birds-eye view of it right outside the bedroom window, beyond with the freshly painted brown steel fire escape.

I knew that I would be traveling at the height of rush hour. This came without the chance or choice of a seat. The ride would be like cattle shoved in a cattle car, or sardines stuffed in a can. It was summer. It would be a miracle if the train I was in had working air-conditioning. It was about a thirty-minute ride into Manhattan and then I had to catch a downtown train. The whole trip would take about forty-five mins; same for the return trip. I got to the building at eighty thirty. My first stop was the bathroom to freshen up, comb my hair, take a deep breath, gather all my thoughts, and even let the butterflies out.

I caught the next sharp-looking polished brass elevator and went up to the sixteenth floor. As I left the elevator, I made a right on impulse and walked about twenty yards down the hall. In large big brown wooden letters, I saw MERRILL, LYNCH, PIERCE, FENNER & SMITH. I walked up to a very impressive thick mahogany desk. With a pleasant smile, the young blond secretary said, "Hi—may I help you?" I told her I had a nine a.m. interview with Mr. DiLeo. She asked if I had my completed application. I gave it to her in a large new manila envelope. She thanked me and told me to have a seat.

I was still somewhat nervous—better than early that morning, though. After about fifteen minutes another very attractive, well-dressed girl, with long black hair and a short skirt, opened a door off to the side. She told me to come with her. As we were walking, she said, "I love your cologne." That's my motivation for cologne. Most times it's a win-win for me. We walked down a hallway, she opened a door and said "Have a seat and Mr. DiLeo will be right with you."

About three minutes later, he appeared. He was around forty-five, not too tall, with thick black hair, a nice smile, and an olive complexion. He had a real nice suit, a matching tie, and a diamond ring on his right pinky. He extended his hand, introduced himself, and complimented me on my strong handshake. First impressions were on the money.

He began by saying, "I hear you're a good friend of Mary's." With that he added, "She is a great, smart, lovely girl. She is going to go places here." That broke the ice. What he was about to say almost made me jump out of the chair. I got an unbelievable warm rush, from head to toe. "I see here on your application that you lived in Corona. So did I."

Holy shit! At that point, he basically just handed me the job. It was *surreal*.

He started to name names of all the people from the old neighborhood. I knew everyone. He went to St. Leo's, lived a few blocks from me . . . and we just went on and on. It was such a fantastic connection. Corona is one of those places where no matter where you go, you always run into someone from Corona.

"We could talk all day, Frank," he said. "So when can you start?" I said I had to give the hospital at least two weeks' notice, He said fine. He described the job as being in the "clearing department." I would learn how to balance over-the-counter stock trades. I said, "Fine with me." He got up and, along with a handshake, gave me a huge bear hug. "Welcome aboard!" My first day was June 19, 1978. My first call when I got home was to thank Mary. She said it was her pleasure and wished me luck.

Do you hear that old neighborhood echo again, in this new venture? It would not have been possible without Mary or Mike DiLeo. You can call it karma, I guess, too. I was excited, ready, willing, and able to conquer the chaos of the bulls and the bears—I hoped.

On my first day, I arrived early and had to ask for my supervisor, Mr. Lopez. He promptly came out of his office and officially welcomed me to the clearing department. He had a heavy Hispanic accent. Later on, I heard he was from Cuba. The office, with a succession of large tables, resembled a cafeteria or a bingo hall. At these tables were different groups of ten people each, presumably doing different jobs at each table. He brought me to my group's table. I couldn't help but notice I was the only white person in the group. I quickly remembered that this is exactly how it was at Elmhurst Hospital on my first day. Not a problem.

I caught on pretty quickly to the job functions and responsibilities. It was not sitting at that large table all day. There was a lot of moving around, from going to mail and Xerox rooms to exchanging information with other departments on different floors in the building. I didn't mind moving around. I got to meet and know many people in the other departments, all very nice, hyper people.

I made it through my first day, no problem. If I left at five p.m. and made my train connections, I would get home at around six p.m. Just in time for dinner. As we started to get into the summer months, though, those cattle trains were getting rougher and rougher. I had been diagnosed with a stomach condition called irritable bowel syndrome, around that time. It seemed to flare up in the summer months or when I was in a stressful or anxiety-ridden situation. There was not really any medication for it at that time, just over-the-counter stuff.

On many of those hot summer mornings, I would get an attack on the train. I would break into sweats and as the train would stop at a station I would have to run out and find a bathroom, and fast. It was terrible. Those days, to get into a bathroom stall, you had to put a dime in a slot to open it. You could imagine the amount of dimes I kept in my right pocket. Not pleasant times.

On one particular day, I was thrown a major curveball. I got up to leave at five p.m. I noticed nobody else was moving. One guy said, "Mr. Lopez is not gonna like that." As soon as that was out, Mr. Lopez appeared and asked where I was going. I said home. He said, "No you're not. From now on, I will tell you when you can go home." I did not like that. So you know where I had to go at that point: men's room

You could not even leave the building for lunch or dinner. They would have food brought in. There were nights I was there till eleven p.m. They would send me home in a yellow cab. This was insanity. There were managers who lived in New Jersey and Connecticut who would leave at eleven p.m. or later and be there the next morning at eight a.m. To add insult to injury, you also had to come in on Saturday and Sundays.

I was now hanging by a thread—not a happy camper. I just could not keep this ridiculous pace. One Saturday afternoon, Mr. Lopez exploded on me for some little bullshit. I got really upset and went to the bathroom again. As I was washing my hands under those glaring fluorescent lights, with lots of pink liquid soap, I looked at my face in the mirror and said to myself, *Frank, it's over. I'm outta here!* I just couldn't do it any longer. I went straight to Mr. Lopez's office and told him I did not appreciate the way he confronted me. He said, "Too bad, Mr. Frank." I went right up to him and said "I quit." I walked out of his dusty, disorganized office feeling mentally exhausted and, now delusional, slammed the door behind me.

That was the official end of my Crazy Wall Street career. I also thought about Mike DiLeo. I never spoke to him again. I'm sure he would have helped me, but that life wasn't for me. You live and learn.

I made my way down the elevator, onto the street, and into that hot, dirty, loud subway. It was a long, sad, and lonely train ride home. In a way, I felt defeated. Looking back, I should have given it more thought, tried to stick it out. I felt forced to make a regretful, impulsive decision.

The good part was the air-conditioning was actually working on the train and all the cattle seemed to be long gone. The bad part was I was out of a job: no income, no, benefits and a new baby on the way. "Oh Boy"! I was thinking about what could possibly be the next trick I would be able to pull out of a hat.

CHAPTER XI

HISTORY REPEATS ITSELF & YOU'RE NOT MY FATHER

When my Father had his railroad injury, he was out of work for nearly two years. It all came gushing back from my memory bank. Here I was: three kids and one on the way, the breadwinner but not being able to bring home any bread. Just like my old Corona days with no safety net, always waiting for the other shoe to drop. I could only wish and hope that we would be able to receive the tremendous outpouring of love and support and generosity that my parents got back in the late 1960s.

Carmen was still getting State Aid. She received a notice that since her name had changed and she had remarried, she would have her case temporarily suspended. She had to reopen her case with my information incorporated. It was a red-tape, drawn-out process. The bottom line was that we were shortly expecting a new baby and time was of the essence. We now had no medical insurance and no income. I told her that we should go to Flushing Hospital, where she would deliver, and speak to social services. We made an appointment and in a day or so were able to speak with them. Our case worker was Mr. Joseph Pasqualino. I liked the sound of his name off the bat. We told him our story and he said he would try his best to help us out.

During the sit-down we came to realize that me and Joe had some similarities. His family came from the same town that my ancestors did in Italy. He had relatives from Corona. He loved and frequently visited the Lemon Ice King. I told him I lived right down the block from there.

He told us to give him about a week to submit all the necessary paperwork. He would call us as soon as he had some information. I gave him my usual strong handshake and told him I would greatly appreciate anything he could do for us.

He did call us, like he said. Carm's case got reinstated and, along with it, the medical insurance. He ended the conversation by saying, "I had to take care of you—you're a friend of ours!" Again, we shared a good laugh. Carmen questioned me about that comment, and I said "It's an Italian thing" and left it at that. I can say it again: *there goes that echo!*

Carmen didn't make it to her due date. On a rainy Saturday morning, October 14, 1978 at 5:41 a.m., our big, beautiful baby girl came into the world. Eight pounds, eight ounces, and twenty-two inches long. She and Frankie were both born on a Saturday at the same hospital. Naming the new baby, I wanted to be original, nontraditional. In 1978, there was a popular band called Captain & Tennille.

I just loved how the name *Tennille* flowed and sounded. My grandmother used to call me, *Francanelle*—don't ask me why. It sounded a little feminine to me. Somehow though, it stuck, through all those years. Now I took that name and put *Tanya-* in the front of it: *Tanyanelle*. Carm agreed that it was certainly original and also loved how it sounded. The translation in Italian is *Little Tanya*.

Now, with four kids in a two-bedroom apartment, it was getting tight. Just like in the Corona days, we got a couch that opened up to be a bed. It made things much easier.

I continued to look for a job—unfortunately, with no luck. I was stuck. I had no education, and the only experience I had to offer would be in a medical-clerk capacity. I would buy the three daily newspapers and religiously read the classified sections every morning. It became part of my breakfast.

Our families were super generous during those trying and crying times. I had only witnessed depression in my life up till that point. I now began to experience it. It was very tough. I couldn't let it take me over. I couldn't let those around me see it. I was the captain of my ship. I was determined never, ever, ever to let that ship go down.

Being as she was, Carmen's motto was always, "*The Lord Jesus Christ will take care of us all.*" Born a Roman Catholic, she switched gears and decided to join the Pentescostal Church. She would attend different churches and religious groups all over the city, mostly on the weekends. The groups consisted mostly of Latina women . I was never on board with all of her religious happenings, interests, or gatherings. This would eventually lead to a number of our philosophical differences. She would constantly be reading the Bible while I was reading *Sports Illustrated*.

Myrna and Maria were now starting high school. It would just so happen to be at my alma mater, Newtown. They both played varsity sports; Myrna played softball and Maria did gymnastics. I tried to go see them play as much as I could. During one of Myrna's games, she severely injured her left ankle. She was very discouraged, afraid that the injury would take quite some time to heal. Her coach was gracious enough to bring her home. I then carried her on my back up four flights of steps up to our apartment.

At that time, the girls started to spread their wings and find their individual identities. I saw contrasting choices. Maria gravitated towards being what I saw as a follower. Myrna was more of a leader.

The relationship between me and the girls was starting to sour. I guess their maturity had a lot to do with it. At one point, Maria began to use the phone at liberty. At all hours of the night. I told her that she would have to ask me or her mother for permission. With that she turned to me and vehemently shouted, "*You're not my father!*"

I said, "I know I'm not; you don't have to remind me, either." The next day I put a lock on the phone. Case closed.

During the beginnings of a tumultuous environment, Myrna decided to write a letter to her mother. I guess she found it easier to put on paper what she had to say. It was so profound and upsetting; it was also extremely poignant She said that she and her sister were never in favor of the marriage. *You never ever considered our feelings. He was much too young. You were very vulnerable and selfish. We never had the heart to tell you. Now it's about time.* Needless to say, Carm was bewildered, devastated and heartbroken. Many sleepless nights followed her.

Myrna went on to Buffalo State University after high school. Maria graduated the following year and also went on to Buffalo. Not to college, though; she got a job with a large medical-supply company.

All the animosity that was accumulating in those times put an enormous strain on our marriage. Even though we now just had too small kids to concentrate on, the challenges persisted. I could see that Carmen was never really the same after the girls left. To add to the growing resentment, Carm's health issues started to escalate. So did our many differences.

I began to notice her insecurity level was on the rise. Did it all stem from the letter?

I would do my best moving forward while trying to keep the ship afloat.

CHAPTER XII

GOT A JOB IN A WOMEN'S WORLD & THE BEES WERE A BUZZIN'

As we entered a new decade, the next course of events would change my life forever. It was apparent that the marriage would need some type of mending. I knew that there were bridges to cross, mountains to climb.

As a young boy, given the extremely difficult childhood that I was forced to navigate, I had this recurring dream. I would feel a sensation of free-falling and never landing. The interpretation by the authors of dreams would classify that meant four things: insecurity, instability, anxiety, and a general feeling of overwhelmedness. Looking back, all were perfectly true to form.

On my journey, I had a vivid image of just what had to be accomplished in order to achieve success. It would be that stick-with-it-ness that would provide the building blocks that would ultimately give me the strength to overcome any adversities to the best of my abilities.

In 1980, the world witnessed some of the most exciting events in history. Unfortunately, there was one event that was tragic, unexpected, and would really rock the world—and rock and roll. On December 8th, a poet, author, activist, and music legend, John Lennon, was shot and killed as he entered his apartment building, The Dakota in New York City. He was only forty.

In technology, the camcorder and the fax machine were invented. Pac-Man and the Rubik's Cube were born. The big movie was *The Empire Strikes Back*. Japan became the world's leader in the auto industry.

On one particular day, I picked up the *New York Times*. It had to be for the first and last time. I immediately went to the classified section and looked at the section that said *Hospital and Medical Positions*.

I came across something that said "Long Island Jewish Hospital in New Hyde Park seeks a Medical Clerk." Wow! That certainly caught my attention in a flash. I figured, this is the closest position that I have seen to being compatible with my experience. I got a resume together, followed the instructions, and mailed it at the post office that afternoon. I had nothing to lose.

I was very familiar with the hospital. Working in the field for some years, you get to know and hear about all other local hospitals. Long Island Jewish had the distinction of being very prestigious and also being located on the actual border line of Queens and Nassau County, Long Island.

After about a week, to my surprise, I received a letter stating that they had received my resume and would like to set up an interview. A representative would contact me. I got a call right after the letter. *Is this really happening?* was circling throughout my head.

It was a twenty-minute drive from Jackson Heights. I got there a little early, just to take in the sights. It was on a beautiful sprawling campus, with fresh green grass, an array of different trees, and colorful flowers. A far cry from the crowded, dreary, colorless grounds of where I used to work at Elmhurst Hospital. The interview went very well. The position was for a tumor registrar in the federally funded cancer program. The woman interviewing me went on to explain that the purpose of this new program was basically to provide information for research. She asked if I was interested and I said absolutely.

She said that she would get back to me with a decision. The interview was over. She thanked me for my interest and I replied, "The pleasure was mine!"

The only thing that was missing from the interview was my signature handshake. That would be okay. I had very strong and positive feelings that I interviewed well. It was a pleasant ride home. I missed those beautiful surroundings already. I just had a good feeling that I would be calling Long Island Jewish my home away from home for a long time. My premonitions were usually on the money.

I told Carmen all about the job and the interview. She seemed to like what she heard. After a week, I received the letter of acceptance. It was contingent upon a physical and drug test. My start date was February 4, 1980. I was very excited to get back to work and finally lift that black cloud I was living under. I had this strong wave of confidence, a feeling that everything would be alright.

The hours were eight to four, Monday to Friday. I arrived on my first day at seven thirty a.m. The dress code was business casual. The department was located in a trailer (I found out later on, that a state-of-the-art cancer building was in the plans for the future). As I entered the trailer, there was a woman at the front desk. She said, "You must be Frank Marotta!" From her accent, she sounded like she was from the West Indies. Her name was Laverne. She welcomed me aboard and said that she was the Supervisor.

She went on to give me a picture of what the cancer program was all about. The two main players were doctors of oncology: Dr. Arthur Sawitsky and Dr. Kanti Rai. The other members of the team were a nurse practitioner, a Nutritionist, a social worker, a news-media representative, a data-process manager . . . and two other tumor registrars. She spoke very highly of the team and added that they were all wonderful professionals. She continued on to say that the program was an integral part of the cancer community. Doctors and clinicians would request different studies on all the different types of cancer. The results of these studies would appear in local and national medical journals and publications. Very impressive, I thought.

She really covered all the bases. She then brought me into the office where the two registrars were and where I would be working. "Girls, I want you to meet Frank." They both got up and extended their hands as they welcomed me. At that point, Laverne left the office and closed the door behind her.

I sat in between two female bookends. On my left was Middy. She was Hispanic from Colombia. On my right was Adrianna, a light-skinned Black woman. I could see we'd all made very positive first impressions. It was now a feeling-out process between us. The sort of, "Okay, let's get to know each other." It didn't bother me at all. The first question they asked was if I were married. I said yes. The next question was, what nationality is your wife? When I said Puerto Rican, Middy said "Oh my lord." I questioned her remark, and she answered, "My husband is Puerto Rican, and we are having real issues. I thought that was a very peculiar remark to make to someone you just met. She added that in her opinion, Puerto Rican women have the reputation of being jealous, possessive, and vindictive. I just said "Oh, okay. . . ." I didn't know what else to say. I was trying to sort out what her motive was.

As the conversations continued, I surmised that Adrienne was a couple of years younger than me and Middy a couple of years older. Adrienne was apparently looking for love, and Middy was apparently done with love. Middy had no filter. Adrienne was much more polished and reserved. They both had a great sense of humor, though. We hit it off very well and quickly. We enjoyed many laughs along the way.

After the non-job-related questions and gossip session, they begin to explain the functions of a registrar. I could quickly see that it would all be on-the-job training for me. I also noticed that I was the only male in the trailer. That did not bother me in the slightest.

So I successfully began my new career and became one of the girls—figuratively, that is. Back home, I faced an interrogation.

You would think the first question would be "How was your first day?" It was not. Even after I volunteered most of the answers before being asked, I could see what direction Carm's mind was taking her. Especially when I said I was the only guy in the office. I believed Her insecurities were knocking at the door again. The problem was, she kept on answering.

CHAPTER XIII

MR. MOM CONTINUES TO MANAGE IT ALL

I thought that a family vacation would be a great idea. It would be a good distraction. I decided on Pennsylvania. It would have to be short and inexpensive. I figured a long weekend would work. Frankie was now six and Tanyanelle was four. Good ages, I thought, for the kids to experience their first vacation. It was the summertime, so the weather would cooperate.

There was a place called Dutch Wonderland I'd heard good things about. It was all kid-friendly. It was also in the Amish country, which was a tourist spot. I thought the kids would like to see that. It was a plan. As we got close to our destination, the kids were amazed at all the beautiful shades of green countryside, with its gazing cows, horses, and other animals that happened to be around. The looks on their faces were magical. There is something so special in a kid's face the first time they see or experience something. This was certainly one of those moments.

The kids just loved and were absolutely amazed at all the things to do and see in Dutch Wonderland. We also went on a tour of an Amish house, school, and church. They were mesmerized. We ate in an authentic country place along with the other tourists. There were farm stands in abundance, selling farm-fresh, locally grown fruits and vegetables all day long. Again something the kids had never seen. It was also their first time in a hotel. They got a kick out of it. .

We had a great time. I set out to do something good for the kids and also to have a change of pace for me and Carmen. I think I accomplished both. That vacation would sadly be our first and last.

Not only was I the breadwinner in our household, I was also the bread maker. Carm's physical challenges were mounting..For her, the challenges that came with our relationship from the get-go—primarily the age difference, the cultural differences , and the sudden unexpected pregnancy—started to slip through the cracks and come front and center.

Physically, she had a history of asthma, migraines, and many gynecological issues. You can mix in some anxiety as well. I would gather These chronic maladies, most of the time, preventing her from doing some normal household chores. She required a lot of down time. The only time she would seem to get a window or a ray of light and energy was on Sundays, when she would attend her Church services. Where she found peace and serenity, she would profess.

Me being me, I would in no way shape or form expect the household to suffer on multiple levels. "I'll do it" became my mantra. She knew very well of all of my capabilities.

When the kids were young, they always preferred me to do things with them. From giving baths, to changing diapers, to feedings, to tying shoes, to combing hair. You name it. It became comical when they used to say "Daddy do it!"

Looking back, it was all a great experience with the kids for me. Being so young at the time, I felt that I was actually growing up just like they were. You have to remember, I never experienced any of that with my own parents, sad as it sounds. I lived my entire childhood missing out on so many things. I made sure that when I had kids, that was not gonna happen.

I noticed That my little wizard, Frankie, acquired a new interest. On our Block there was always an abundance of cars. It resembled a parking field. A we many times would walk up and down, Frankie just started to ask me about the particular cars. He would ask, "Daddy, what kind of car is that?" A pretty unusual question for a six-year-old, I thought. So I would go on to tell about all the different years, makes, and models of all the cars we would see. This went on for a while. Before you knew it, I would ask him about certain cars. He would actually give me the year, make, and model. Just incredible. I could see instantly he had a love of and passion for cars. There wasn't really any place for the kids to play, on that busy, hectic block.

At the entrance of our building was a covered walkway that led to a courtyard. In the brick-covered entrance were two different areas to enter the courtyard, which had a big, beautiful fountain in its center. The entranceway had a three-foot brick landing down the center. The kids used to sit there and make up games or congregate and find ways to laugh and just have fun. They liked that entranceway cause they could still be there even if it rained.

On this particular day, Frankie went down to play with the kids. There was this one kid, Harvey, who was a known bully. He was actually smaller than most of the other kids. He also had the biggest foul mouth. Just a real pain-in-the-ass kid. Would easily get under someone's skin.

After about fifteen minutes, Frankie rang the bell. I stuck my head out the double kitchen window and said, "What's the matter?" He looked up and I could see he was crying. I told him to wait there and I would be right down. I got there and I asked him what happened. He hesitated and said, "Harvey hit me!" I asked why, and Frankie said, "I don't know why."

I said, "Here is what you're gonna do. You are gonna go up to Harvey, you are not gonna say anything. All you are gonna do is, with all your might, punch him right in his face."

"No, no, Daddy, I can't do that!"

"Listen to me. If you don't do what I'm telling you, you will go upstairs and you will not come out to play with your friends for the whole week."

He looked me in the eye and said "Okay."

The stage was set. I was a few paces behind him as he slowly went towards Harvey. Harvey was sitting on the landing like a little dictator, holding court in front of all the kids. Frankie raised his right arm as far back as it could go and landed a tremendous overhand right to Harvey's face. The force knocked the little bastard right off the landing, to the ground. He got up, dazed and confused, wobbling slowly a few doors down to his apartment building. He was hunched over and looking down, noticeably defeated before his followers.

Frankie turned around and slowly walked away with his chest out, head up, and shoulders back, beaming with confidence. He met me at our entrance steps. I got down on my right knee so we could be eye to eye. I asked him how he now felt. His answer was "*Great.*" I explained to him the meaning of a bully. I could see in his eyes he was a little confused but eventually got my drift. The moral of the story was my great little boy was not only now loved by his peers, he was also feared. I gave him a big kiss on his check and hugged him tight. We went upstairs and I made him his favorite lunch.

One of Carm's church friends' daughters was getting married, and we were invited to the wedding. I had never met these people. They were from the Dominican Republic. I thought it would be something nice for us to do, since we never did anything alone. Aunt Gertie watched the kids for us.

We went to the church ceremony and the reception immediately followed. When we walked into a very decorated hall that featured the biggest collection of red-and-white balloons I have ever seen I quickly noticed that I was the only non-Hispanic person in the entire place. That goes also with the only English as a first language person too. It was a weird feeling.

I never in my life saw so many beautiful women under one roof. They were very impressive. I'm sure that Carm took notice of what I was taking notice of. I was only human. There was also a live band playing. They were very good. Like most latin women, Carmen was a great dancer. I on the other hand, I had two left feet. Kind of embarrassing. I could just never get the friggin rhythm down. I must say though, in my defense, I could carry a tune pretty well.

The reception came to an end. It was a rather unexpectedly good time. The food and the drinks were all top shelf. I just wished I could have communicated with the other guests better. I had to constantly ask Carm, "What did they say?" The night was over, as the overhead lights began to dim. We wished the bride and groom good luck. Carm had to say goodbye to all of her friends. I just kept nodding my head, like a jerk. It was good to go outside and get some air. The place had been a little stuffy. No air conditioning.

On the ride home, Carm blurted something out of her mouth that would have rocked any husband's senses who had just left a wedding with his wife. "I bet you were thinking about screwing all of those beautiful women at the wedding! Am I right? Tell me the truth!"

I literally almost had to pull the car over. I was flabbergasted. I answered, "*What the fuck are you talking about!?*" This would be the beginning of an assortment of I thought outlandish, irrelevant, irrational off-the-wall comments she would come out with. She followed all that up with another bizarre scenario. I guess she thought she was on a roll.

This one was a classic I must say. In Puerto Rico, she heard, I guess it was an old wive's tale or folklore that if a wife found out that her husband was having an affair or suspected him, while in bed in the middle of the night she would wake him up and tell him she needed sex—and fast. When the husband was fully aroused, she would take a sharp knife or razor blade from under her pillow and cut his manhood off.

I couldn't help but think that moving forward, maybe one day, I hoped not, I would have to sleep with one eye open.

All the crazy things that would come out of her or lack thereof made me believe a few things. First, she was extremely underestimating me . She began to show unnecessary signs of defensiveness, possessiveness and a sort of a weird weakness. Above all, a continued downward spiral into insecurity. Where were these feelings and thoughts coming from? I never, ever gave her any rhyme or reason to question my fidelity. Or anything else, for that matter. I had no clues. I was starting to actually believe that she was trying to create an environment or a tone that would be extremely difficult for me to accept or understand or to survive in. All of this I predicted would lead to really eventually damaging our relationship. Here I was trying to do the right thing, not to mention be a pretty damn good father and husband for that matter. It became overbearing, frustrating, and daunting, to say the least.. I started to think of my father and how he dealt with my mother all those early crazy years. If only I could have asked him for advice.

CHAPTER XIV

MY PATIENCE AT HOME CONTINUED TO DEPLETE & MY PATIENTS AT WORK WERE COMPLETELY DEPLETED

In 1982, *Time Magazine* named the computer the "Person of the Year." Sonny's Compact Disc Player (CD) made its debut in Japan. Designer Calvin Klein's first underwear ad stopped traffic in Times Square. *E.T. the Extra Terrestrial* became the largest-grossing film in the United States. Michael Jackson's album *Thriller* became the best-selling album of all time.

When I got to Jackson Heights in 1974, the neighborhood was basically all Irish and German immigrants. As time progressed, an influx of South American neighbors, predominantly from Colombia, came in and changed the face of the neighborhood. They also brought the drug trade with them. Over time it got so rampant that Jackson Heights became known as the "cocaine capital of the world."

The undocumented immigrants that were coming in very large groups had plans to avoid the authorities at any cost. Women would offer American men $10,000 to marry them and have their child. This loophole would make them and their babies citizens. A lot of that was going on; I saw it firsthand in my building. The area quickly became undesirable. There was crime, robberies, and murders everywhere.

Carmen continued her quest to demonstrate jealous streaks, false accusations, and prevailing insecurities. She perplexed me to no end. She couldn't realize that she was slowly pushing me away. She also got deeper and deeper into her religious practices.

Our basic at-home conversations now became very unproductive and argumentative.

It was just all so baffling to me. She was constantly searching for this delusional reality that just was never there.

I took the kids with me all the time when I went to the supermarket or did the laundry or just local errands. They love it. Tanyanelle would often go with her mother to the church functions on Sunday. Me and Frankie would watch baseball, basketball, hockey, football, depending on the season. I just kept on thinking and believing that I was holding up my end of the marriage. I always had a calm exterior and was extremely passive in those trying and difficult days. What was going on inside me was another story. Plus I had severe stomach issues.

My new job, though, was going great. I picked it up pretty quick. I became fascinated by all the medical jargon and the actual process of how and why there is this dreadful disease called cancer. I got attached to my two bookend girls. It was fun going to work. We got along so well. When we just spoke about life's trials and tribulations, there was nothing held back. When they heard about what I did in my household, they were shocked. I told them I was very hands on.

Middy was constantly complaining about her husband. Adrienne met a nice guy, a lawyer, and believed that he was the one she had been searching for.

The girls told me that one of the job requirements in the tumor registry was traveling. You would have to go on follow-up field trips and attend seminars and conferences. I thought that all would be interesting. The first trip we went on was to the Bureau of Vital Records, in the city.

Our purpose was to look at the death records of patients that we had lost contact with in the registry. It was very time-consuming and tedious. We made the best of it by having a great lunch at our own pace in the big city. The highlight of the day was when I stumbled across some valuable information: The department also housed New York State birth records. The particular birth record that I saw was of ROSARIA YANNUCCI born in CORONA NEW YORK, September 10, 1926. My mother!

We got an invitation to Adrienne's wedding. We were planning to go and my mother was to watch the kids. The day of the wedding, Carmen spent about three hours getting ready with her clothes, shoes, hair, and makeup.

I had my suit on and the kids were all dressed and ready to go. I made it known that it was getting late and she needed to pick up her pace. She said she didn't like the way her hair was coming. I told her again that we had to get going. This time I got loud. She then said I was rushing her. I said, "You're in the mirror for over two hours!" She threw down the hair dryer and brush and said, "Now I'm not fucking going."

I could not believe what she had just said. I yelled, *"You have to be kidding me!"* What I should have done was say "Fine, I'll go by myself." But I couldn't. Again, that's the way I was. I was so distraught and humiliated. I took my suit off and went to my mother's. I needed to calm down. When I got there, I told her the whole story. She said, "Oh my god, that is so terrible." I wrote Adrianna a nice letter explaining why I wasn't there. It was an embarrassing time. I enclosed it with her gift in the wedding card.

I got to know a lot of people in the hospital, especially in security. Most of the guys were Italian. There was one who stood out;

everyone in the hospital knew him. Lieutenant Babino. A very funny and warm character. He actually lived in Elmhurst. I told him I was from Corona, and he said he knew a lot of people there. He was retired from the New York City Department of Sanitation, where he had been a supervisor for many years. He would be a good guy to know, with all his contacts. I later found out later that his granddaughter Cathy worked in the ambulatory accounting department.

The entire staff of the cancer program was to meet one day in the main conference room of the main hospital. No one had a clue why. The news we were about to hear was not good. Dr. Sawitsky informed us that the program lost its federal funding. It was to be terminated immediately. We were all shocked and stunned. It was like a family death.

The next day we all had to go back to the trailer and clean out our stuff. It was a very sad day for us. There were many hugs and tears to go around. Most went back to their previous departments. The new tumor registry was limited to just two people: Adrienne and Laverne. Middy decided to go to nursing school. Dr. Kanti Rai went on to become a worldwide authority in the science of all blood-related Cancers.

It was a great experience for me to have been associated with such awesome medical professionals. It paved the way for me to pursue my goal to further my medical education. I didn't know where my next destination would be in the hospital. My Union Local 1199 would take care of placing me. Something told me that wherever I was going, It was going to be a pretty nice place to work.

CHAPTER XV

SCIENCE & RELIGION IN THE FACE OF POSSIBLE LIFE AND DEATH

In 1983, IBM released the first PC XT. Microsoft Word was launched. The Space Shuttle Challenger made its maiden flight. On board was Sally Ride, the first American woman in space. The video game Mario Bros. was introduced. The Cabbage Patch Kids hit the toy market. Richard Noble sets the new land speed record of 633.468 mph. Barney Clark becomes the first recipient of an artificial heart in the United States. He expired after 112 days.

The marriage continued to slide down a slippery slope. Carmen seemed somewhat oblivious to the whole thing. We were for sure on different spectrums. I remained optimistic and had my sights on succeeding. The issue remained, though, that with no mutual effort, my plight would remain futile. Carm decided she wanted to add something that in her mind, would ease all the tension and hostilities that were floating in our airways.

After our many arguments and disagreements, she wanted to turn to some strong acts of intimacy. I thought it was weird. She probably thought that being physically attached would bring us closer in other areas, to be sort of a cure-all. I guess it was a defense mechanism. I would beg to differ.

She made an appointment to see her gynecologist. She'd missed her cycle for a few weeks, but that was normal. They were always very erratic. I sat in the waiting room for forty-five minutes. When she came out, she had this perplexed, weird look on her face. I didn't want to ask her any questions until we got into the car. When I finally asked, she replied, "I'm pregnant!"

I said, "What!?" She said it again. "*Jesus Chris almighty,*" I said. I didn't mean it in a religious way. I just wanted to scream and jump out of my sneakers. I was more than livid. It wasn't really the kind of news I wanted to hear. Given our current circumstances.

I immediately had a flashback to when she'd uttered those same exact words to me back in July of 1975. So here we are, in an unpredictable shakey marriage, with our backs against the wall. How many times would I have to be tested in my relatively young life? Those thoughts encompassed my being. Due to her age, her health and probably her escalating stress levels, the doctor told her that she would have to have an amniocentesis, a test that checks the amniotic fluid of the fetus, with the purpose of ruling out any birth defects and or chromosomal abnormalities..

The test was to be done in the hospital. She got an appointment a few weeks later. After we absorbed all this new upside-down predicament, we decided not to tell any family or friends about it. We didn't even tell the kids. Given the state of things, the underlying message here was, in my pessimistic mind, I would be in favor of not going through with the pregnancy. Carm, on the other hand, with her strong religious beliefs, would under no circumstance whatsoever, be in favor of my wishes. None of this was going to be easy. Time would tell.

Back at work, I'd found out what department I was going to: the ambulatory accounting department. It was in the finance building, the farthest part away from the main building. It had its own cafeteria, so we didn't have to go to the main hospital for lunch. From my first day, I could see that I was going to be one of the girls again, figuratively. The manager and the supervisor were both women. I noticed only four other guys. The rest of the office was full of at least forty women with an age gap from around twenty-five to sixty-five.

They were of all shapes, sizes, and nationalities. In my mind, I put the office in three categories: young, middle-aged, and old. The three other guys were in a separate office, off the main office. That's where I would work from too. It just so happened that outside my office would be where the young-girl crew all sat. I figured it would take some time to get to know everyone. The good thing was that everyone had an ID badge on. It made it a little easier just to learn everyone's name.

As I could see, right outside my office sat Cathy Babino. Not only was she the best-looking one in the entire office, I put two and two together and realized that she was Lieutenant Babino's granddaughter—the guy I'd met in security. The first chance I got, I introduced myself and said, "Your grandfather works in security?" She said yes. I told her I met him and we spoke on occasion. It kind of broke the ice. Cathy was the first girl I spoke to in the office. Excellent first impression. I thought.

The guys were all really nice. It seemed that Don, the other white guy, was older than me. I was older than the two Black guys, Ron and Trevor. There was another guy that worked amidst all the girls. His name was Lee. Lee and Don were real big sports fans. We even played on the hospital softball team. I really enjoyed it. The department was a far cry from the cancer program experience I got. I would now be exposed to the financial aspects of a hospital, a fine learning experience.

Carmen's crucial exam was upon us. We had to go to the radiology-special-procedure department at Flushing Hospital. I had taken off from work so I could take her to the nine-a.m. appointment. Waiting, I just felt that this whole process was not gonna turn out well. She had too many things stacked up against her. Her age, all the medical issues, and her stress level. All not very conducive. To a productive pregnancy. The procedure took about an hour. My thoughts and the suspense of it all consumed me to no end. The doctor told us that we would know in a week what the results would be. The office would call us at that time and we would meet him again for a consultation.

My mind was working in overdrive that entire week when we got the call for the appointment. It was for a late afternoon. I left work early. We got to the office and were called right in. We sat in front of the large, solid dark wood desk, both nervously and patiently waiting for the Doctor and the highly anticipated results.

He came in with a lab coat over his blue suit and red tie. He had what seemed to be the results in a large folder under his left arm. "Okay," he began. " Unfortunately the results that we have are not good. The fetus has severe chromosomal damage which ultimately will lead to chronic and very serious abnormalities. The prognosis is very bleak. Life expectancy would remain an issue.

The news began to sink in and fast. Carm just gazed into space as she wiped the tears from her eyes. The doctor gave his recommendation: to terminate the pregnancy. Carm at that point said, "This is now in the hands of my Lord and Saviour Jesus Christ"!

The doctor told us that the decision was entirely up to us. "Unfortunately," he added, "time is of the essence. You have till the twenty-fourth week of the pregnancy to decide. After that, you must go full term. Which also is not a guarantee."

She was at about twenty-two weeks at that point. We left the office and pondered those two very short, crucial weeks—the longest short weeks of my life. There was complete silence on the car ride home. I asked her when we got home, "How can you bring a life into this world that basically has no life?"

She insisted that *God would take care of it all*. In the twenty-third week, she woke up in the middle of the night cramping and bleeding pretty badly. When we got to the emergency room, they sent her directly up to Labor and Delivery. She was in a lot of pain. After about two hours, she eventually miscarried.

They called me into the room; Carmen was crying hysterically. I did my best to console her. The doctor said she would stay the night. It was a sad tragic ending, but also truly a miracle that the termination never did happen. Somebody was looking after her.

I didn't know what to expect moving forward, as far as how this all would affect Carm. I thought I had seen all her sides. All I knew was that I was drained physically and mentally and emotionally. I didn't know how much more I could really endure.

I had to dig deeper than I ever had before. I needed answers. I did not know where all of this was headed. I felt I would have to look at and most likely be in a position, to make life altering decisions not only for me but my family as well. Like I always said, "I'm not religious"! When I went to sleep that night, I looked up and just asked for HELP.

CHAPTER XVI

A STALKER, A CRUCIAL DECISION & MOMMY DEAREST MAKES A COMEBACK

I found myself constantly making some pretty hefty decisions at a relatively young age. The next one I would have to make could very well be my biggest. What to do about our marriage? It would take an enormous amount of intestinal fortitude to come to a conclusion. It's one thing to have a marriage fail. It's another issue when two young kids' lives are also at stake.

My kids were everything to me. They gave me a special opportunity as a parent: to give them a childhood very far from the one that I was unfortunately subject to. But at this juncture, all of it sadly may have to change. It would be my decision. No divorce or separation is ever easy for any child at any age. There will always be ramifications. I would give it my all to minimize whatever trauma I could in the process, if I so had to.

A little consolation was that the kids were only five and seven. Their comprehension would be limited. Kids are resilient. In my heart and soul, I would never ever abandon them. I would always be nearby physically as well as emotionally. I also knew that no matter what, the kids' best interest would always be at hand. That would be a given for us as parents. I would be prepared for any and everything.

After Carmen lost the baby, with her forever revolving door of irrationalities, I would never know exactly where she was coming from. All I knew was I felt like I was hanging off that same mountain from which I had that recurring dream as a kid. I basically sat Carm down in the kitchen after dinner one night and told her how I was feeling. I suggested that we separate for a while. To just regroup and recharge the batteries. I could see in her eyes and body language, that she was very surprised, and she took a step back. She had been living on complacency too long with me and the marriage.

In my mind, I would be giving her one final chance to prove to me that she wanted to continue. I didn't want to tell her that though. I knew she would not take an ultimatum too lightly. Her capricious behavior just had to go away. No alternatives. The ball was in her court. She would dictate my decision on staying in or out of our relationship. During these times, I was confiding in my mother. I gave her the glum climate, the current atmosphere. Her advice was that I think long and hard about my future. She said that the main concern would be the kids. I told her I totally agreed.

Things at the hospital were going great. I fit in real fast with everyone. There were times that a large part of the office would have lunch together. It was a nice time. Other times it was just the guys. The one constant was that if I was hanging out with the girls, it was definitely the young group. I must say, the office gossip was rampant and entertaining as well.

Since Cathy was the first girl I'd met, our conversations seemed to flow free and easy. The fact that I knew her grandfather created a certain comfort level. I quickly took notice that she was very different from most of the girls in her group. Very middle-of-the-road. A sharp dresser as well. But still mellow and on the reserved side. As our conversations continued, there were some welcoming and surprising parallels. You could say, *It's a small world after all.*

Cathy was born on the exact day and year as my younger twin brothers Johnny and Joey: September 24, 1959. We had both gone to Newtown High, had some of the same teachers. She knew a lot of kids at Newtown that were from Corona, whom I also knew. Cathy's father's first cousin and her husband Rocky lived in Corona. My father and Rocky had been best of friends for many years and were active together in our church, St. Leo's. Cathy's parents spent a lot of time back in the 1960s in all of Corona's great Italian specialty stores. Cathy remembers, as a kid, getting Italian ice from the Lemon Ice King of Corona, which was right on my corner. She also remembers the Italian Feast of Our Lady of Mount Carmel on 52nd Avenue— she went to as a kid. All these comparisons kept hitting high notes. It was both entertaining and refreshing.

Cathy knew I was married. I asked her if there was a lucky guy in her life. She said yes, for about three years now. I asked her if she had any future plans with her boyfriend. She kind of hesitated and said, "We'll see." She went on to tell me that both of her parents were Italian but born in the United States. I said, mine also. Her grandparents lived with them. So did mine. She was the oldest of three girls and lived in Elmhurst, the boarding town of Corona. Like myself, she had gone to Catholic School for eight years. Our backgrounds were mirror images. Pretty wild and, at the same time, interesting.

Carm knew very well of my office being predominantly full of women. Again, me being naive, I was giving her fuel for the fire. She would call my office two or three times a day with really unimportant subject matters. She used those calls like a telescope, I would perceive. I would have to go to the reception desk to get the calls. Between all the times she use to call and, I guess, the many different expressions on my face, a gossip topic arose amongst the girls. I could just feel it in the air. "*What the hell is this poor guy's wife calling him all the time for?*"

My car had broken down and was in need of some major repairs. I wouldn't have it back in a few days. I guess Cathy overheard me telling one of the guys. She came up to me and said "Would you need me to pick you up?" Wow! I told her that would be *awesome*. So for three days, she picked me up and brought me back home in her blue 1977 Chevy. (Another crazy similarity was that we both drove and liked Chevys.) She saved me from an hour and a half commute with two trains and a bus. All the girls complimented Cathy on how it was such a nice gesture. I totally agreed. I had told Carm that a girl from the office would be able to take me to work. She didn't basically say anything about it all. Ok.

It was a cloudy, dreary Friday afternoon at work as everyone anticipated the welcoming weekend. It was one o'clock and I made my way down to the cafeteria for lunch. Surprisingly, no one from my department was around, so I took a spot at a smaller table. I didn't mind that I was alone. I had my *New York Post* with me so I could read up on all the sports of the weekend.

As you got down to the cafeteria from my floor, there were two gray-slotted metal circular staircases. All of a sudden, I heard what sounded like high heels hitting the steps, each footfall making a pronounced sound against the metal. The heels hitting the steps resembled a military structured cadence. Something told me I would exactly know who was in those high heels.

I followed the sound as it now hit the brown and tan cafeteria floor. I felt the blood rush to my head, my stomach rumbling, my heart pounding out of my chest, my legs became weak. I'm telling myself, *This is not really happening. This cannot be true!* Wearing a tight red dress, mid-thigh, face and hair done like someone was attending a grand-ballroom affair, or having a professional screen test, with red spiked high heels, her opening line was, "Where are all your girlfriends?"

I stood up and said, "Listen, this is a very bad move. You better get the hell out of here before it's too late." She said defiantly, "I'm not going anywhere." This was her antic of all antics. I thought I had seen them all! She just took the life right out of me. Forget about finishing my lunch or my newspaper; they both went right in the first trash can I saw. So did my appetite. I then asked where the kids were.

I knew her strategy. She had all intentions of publicly humiliating me in front of my peers. As my patience level was drained and bad thoughts flooded my head, I thought the best thing to do was to walk away. It was a tough thing to do. I must have had some look on my face when I got back up to my office.. A few people asked if I was alright. I said I'd be fine. I closed the office door and told my friend Don what had just happened. He was dumbfounded, could not believe what had just happened. Outside my office were twelve-foot high glass windows. As I told him, we noticed Carmen peering through the tall windows. I could not believe my eyes; neither could Don. She would stand there for a good thirty minutes.

Little by little, this scene right out of a movie was now being watched by the entire office. The office manager wanted to see me in her office and wanted to know what was going on. She thought it was "an embarrassing and terrible thing to do." Cathy asked if I was alright. I told her I was. She suggested that I go home.

When I got home, we had the fight to end all fights. It got very loud and was very close to becoming physical. The kids had to see all of that, and were crying hysterically. "The audacity of you, to come to my job," I proclaimed. "What the fuck were you trying to prove? What did you accomplish!?" She had no answers. I went on and told her that I gave her all the chances in the world. I added that she never made any attempt to make things at home work, that she was only interested in her goal of trying to prove my infidelity. Which she never could.

I was now completely done; she'd put the last nail in the coffin. I was now going to make my ultimate decision: to leave. I ran out of options. Sunday was Father's Day. I wanted to be with my kids. I felt terrible that they had to be exposed to all this. I felt even worse leaving on such a special day, one that I always enjoyed and loved. So did the kids.

I waited that night until they went to bed. There was no way in hell I wanted them to see me leave. I gave Rosie an update and told her I was coming back home. Carmen was in the kitchen ironing some my shirts as the tears rolled down her face. As I was getting some of my last things together, Frankie woke up. He came running over to me, hugging my right leg for dear life. He begged me not to go. The brilliant mind that he had quickly caught on to the situation at hand. I did all I could to hold back a large bunch of tears as my heart skipped a beat and started to ache. I told him I was going to grandma's house for a while. I went in and kissed Tanyanelle on the check. She was sound asleep. That image of Frankie holding on to my leg has stayed with me forever and ever.

I had put most of my stuff in two large, black, heavy plastic bags. I had no intentions of taking anything substantial from the apartment. You could say I left with nothing but the shirt on my back.

When I finally left on June 26th 1983 at 9:30 p.m., it was surreal. This was the day I'd feared the most. The mysterious part was that I didn't know if I was ever going back. The only thing that was on my mind, as I went out the door and down those four flights of marble steps, was to call Frankie and Tanyanelle the first thing in the morning and tell them, "Daddy loves you and I will see you real soon".

CHAPTER XVII

TURNING OVER A NEW LEAF & ON MY WAY TO A MEDICAL PROFESSION

In 1940, novelist Thomas Wolfe wrote, "You can't go home again." That axiom stood the test of time. In my particular case, though, it was quite the contrary; my dear mother, Rosie, took me in with open arms. So it seemed. In my new uncharted-waters transition, I knew I could not give in to panic. The abundance of stress that I was living with may have just as well been more than enough to break a lesser person, but I firmly believed that I had the right combination of attributes to stay ahead of the game.

I always anticipated what was approaching around every corner. I had a new confidence that the juices of hope would stir once again. I also was well aware that the only constant in life is change. My journey was temporarily derailed; I wanted it back on track again. I knew of the consequences that I would face. I had learned a lot in the process. I so much wanted a chance at redemption.

When I got back home, the Corona that I once knew was all but gone. No longer was it a tight-knit, predominantly Italian neighborhood. It was now filled with crime, vandalism, graffiti, and an overall disrespect for people and property. No more doors wide open. Now they were locked tight. Even the windows had gates on them. It was ugly. My Mother was even robbed and mugged a few times. There were a few old-school die-hards left like my Mother and Aunt Josie and my mother's godmother across the street We all were concerned with their safety. We suggested that they sell the house. But they had been there their entire lives. They were not going anywhere else. *You can lead a horse to water*, which was what we were dealing with.

For me to be in that same house again was for sure bittersweet. The dysfunction and sadness of a tumultuous childhood was reverberating in my head. As I stood in those very rooms again, just taking in that old familiar scenery, I experienced flashbacks galore. The good part about being home again was getting the opportunity to get to know Rosie anew. She was very far from the disturbed, abusive, overbearing mother that I witnessed as a child. She was now my much-needed serene safety net. She had been alone since Daddy died. I was in good company with questionable circumstances. She was my Mother again, at the crossroads of my life.

A reconciliation was a welcoming sight. We were able to just sit back and rehash the old days and ask why things were the way they were. I was able to unload many repressed feelings that I'd been harboring within me. It was certainly cleansing for my heart and soul.

There was an illuminating discovery, realization, disclosure, that would forever change the way I view my mother. She took me back to those old days and brought me into her complex mind. She went on to explain that most times, she was experiencing out-of-body sensations that she unfortunately had no control of. She said she felt "possessed." She went on to say that she was beaten and abused by her father. All of these monumental disclosures opened my eyes well beyond belief. I respected her honesty, sincerity, and courage in all of our heartfelt exchanges.

My grandfather was still across the hall. He never was the same after grandma died. He barely knew had to boil water. His health was starting to fail. Rosie would become his caregiver. Aunt Josie would also help out. He questioned why I was there. I told him and he said, "Make sure you always take care of your kids." I assured him that I would. Grandpa became more mellow in his old age. The stern tough man was now just a shadow of himself.

It was so great to have the traditional Sunday dinner back in my life again. Those early-morning aromas consuming my being—the frying meatballs and the simmering gravy—brought me way back again. Some of my siblings would come. It was such a great thing for me to have just an awesome support system around me. My entire family was well aware of the enormous task I took on at such a young age. They also knew that I had given—always gave—one-hundred percent to try and make it all work. They were here for me now again at the crossroads.

Back at work, all was going well. I guess I was the hot gossip topic, as everyone knew that I was now separated. Cathy and I continued to uncover many more similarities. I guess we got to know each other's personalities pretty quickly. What stood out about her to me was her levelheadedness. I could see that she was very calm and collected. Don, my coworker said one day that he was going out with Cathy to lunch. I thought he was very lucky. He always spoke very highly of her. When he got back, I asked how it went. He said, "Very well." He told me he got the impression that her relationship with her boyfriend was not where she wanted it to be. Don didn't quite know how to read into it. I guess time would tell.

I began to evaluate my situation and take an inventory on all fronts. I thought it would be a good time to try and better myself careerwise and just with life in general. I always remembered that my grandfather said to all his grandchildren: *If you ever wanted to continue your education, I would be glad to help you.* I just had to find a career path. At the time, diagnostic ultrasound was the big new thing. So I did some research and asked around for some advice. I got nothing but positive feedback.

I found a school that was not too far from the hospital. I called them and made an appointment for an interview. It all sounded great. I could see myself as an ultrasound technician. I spoke to my close friends and family about it. They all encouraged me to go for it. The program would be fifteen months: twelve months in a classroom and a three-month clinical. I would receive sixty college credits, compatible to an associate's degree. This all sounded fantastic.

The classes would be Monday to Friday at night from six to ten. I would just go straight from work. It sounded like a plan.

Now I had to talk to grandpa and hope dementia would not have kicked in yet. He was completely fine with the whole idea. He made my Mother write a check for four thousand dollars. That same school today cost forty thousand. I could not thank GrandPa enough. I could not wait to get started. It was exactly what I needed at that time in my life. It was not easy. Working during the day, school at night, dealing with a separation and making sure I saw the kids on the weekends. Also having my Mother they way I always wanted her to be in my life.

Back in Jackson Heights, the kids got a call from me every night. I didn't have too much dialogue with their mother. We agreed that I would take the kids on the weekends. I was impressed as to the way the kids were adapting. For me to be with them on most weekends was something that they were very used to anyway. I still remained keenly attuned to any possible emotional changes. Tanyanelle wanted a bike. So on one of the first weekends, I bought her the pink bike she always wanted. It was rough when I took the training wheels off. She was very frustrated but soon got the hang of it. Even at a young age, she always had no trouble speaking her mind. She is the exact same way now.

I was bringing Carmen money every two weeks when I got paid. I told her that I would cover all her bills as long as I could. Most times I would meet her down by her outside front door or as I was doubled-parked in front of the building There was really no conversation. One day, though, I did not anticipate what she had in mind. I wondered what was in her bag of tricks. She still could not face the realization that I was gone. She had called me the night before and said she needed to talk—it was important. So I rang the bell and she let me up. I hadn't missed those four flights of steps one bit.

When I got to the apartment door, I rang the bell. It took a few minutes for her to open the door. I knew the kids would be at school. When she opened the door, I could not believe what I saw. She had decided not to wear too many clothes along with an evil look in her eye. Already I didn't think this would end well. She also had a glass of red wine in her hand. Again, NOT A GOOD SCENE.. I immediately said, "What the hell are you doing!?" She said, "When I see you, you are like a big steak and I haven't eaten in three days." I had no time or feelings available to accept the compliment. I told her to put some clothes on or I would leave. She refused. She then made an attempt to come to or at me. I knew where she wanted to go with all of this.

At that instance, I threw the money on the kitchen table and got the hell out of there in a hurry. When I got down to the street, she was screaming from the front bedroom window, "*Frank, Frank, please come back! Please, please, I need you!*" All I could think was that display of total desperation led me to believe she was up to her old tricks again. Very sad. There were two other acts of desperation on display I thought, during the next money exchanges. All I can say is that her bitterness, frustrations, vindictiveness and fearfulness led her to make these last awful, unwise, and impulsive decisions. I said at that point to myself, "The check is in the mail!"

CHAPTER XVIII

AN OFFICIAL ENDING, AN OFFICIAL BEGINNING, AN OFFICIAL TITLE

In 1984, President Ronald Regan defeated Walter Mondale to begin his second term. The AIDS virus was discovered. DNA profiling became a reality. Apple released the Macintosh computer. *Terms of Endearment* won the Oscar for best movie. The most popular toy was the Transformer.

It was a year for me in which things were happening at a very fast, furious, and even fruitful pace. It seemed that I'd spent the last decade making many important, substantial decisions. Whatever they were, there was no turning back. I decided to file for divorce. The legal process took more than the average time—she contested the proceedings. I wasn't a bit surprised. I guess she had intentions of not making things any easier for me and, secondly, of going down fighting. She even hired an Italian lawyer. Go figure.

Cathy decided to call it quits with her boyfriend of four years.. It would become the new gossip topic over at ambulatory accounting. I guess Cathy knew exactly what she wanted in a relationship. She made it known that she was in no rush to make it happen, either.

I was starting to believe not just mentally, but deep inside, that all things were possible. I began to create a vision of a new life. I often heard the phrase, *Visions often become realities*. I firmly believed that. It made me wonder what it would be like if in a relationship, the two people would be in the same boat, rowing in the same direction. It would all translate into a spirit of compromise that would make the relationship more empowering and enriching.

Like I said, things were moving pretty fast. The ducks always seemed to be in precise order with Cathy and me. I wasn't ready to tell the kids what was going on with my life. I still had to keep my antennas up to make sure the kids never had any complications with adjusting. I knew it would not be easy for them. But something just told me everything would turn out right.

I took the kids to their first Yankee game. Being automatic Yankee fans, they absolutely loved it. It was something I had always dreamed of. I wished so much as a kid that I would experience that with my father. It never happened. A good neighbor, Sal, was so gracious to take me and my brother Anthony along with him and his son Thomas—whom Rosie called her sixth son—to our first Yankee game when I was ten. A day that I will never forget. The kids and I also spent a lot of Sundays at Grandma Rosie's for Sunday dinner. The kids enjoyed it immensely. Spending time with grandma was beyond special.

I did take notice on a few occasions a little change in Tanyanelle. Sometimes she did not want to come with me and Frankie. She wanted to be with her mother. I had no issue with that, and I never questioned her. Frankie was the complete opposite. He could not wait to be with his pops. Tanyanelle was always original, just like her namesake.

Back at school! I was doing surprisingly well. The subject matters were very intense. I just became a sponge with a vast array of the knowledge. Medicine was my passion. The classroom part was coming to an end; I had to get ready for the internship. I would have to make arrangements at work, because the internship was during the day. I would have to work nights. It all worked out; I was able to get a job in the medical-records department.

Current life began to take on some ironic and peculiar parallels to my past. Some ten years prior, I began to undertake a relationship with an older woman who had two kids. Cathy now found herself in a relationship with an older guy who had two kids. A coincidence indeed. Just as my parents hadn't approved of the relationship, neither did Cathy's parents. Some of the same obstacles would persist. Weird. The circle of life, I guess.

As we dated, I realized that among other things, I had the opportunity to relive the teenage years I never had. With Cathy, we went to shows, concerts, theatre, bars, restaurants, parties. She gave me a second chance to capture those very important years of my life. My confidence was now alive. She gave me so many other intangibles. We were communicating effortlessly. It was free and easy, with two feet on the ground. I guess I had to get used to the wonder of it all. Not always waiting for the other shoe to drop.

My internship was about to begin. I had finished the classroom part with a ninety-percent average. I was now in a hospital in an outpatient-clinic setting. My mentor was a guy named Steve. He was a masterful ultrasound technician. I just loved and appreciated his brilliance. He was also an accomplished pianist, so we had a lot in common with our love for music. I began to scan on a regular basis. I was doing abdominal, obstetric, and gynecologic studies. I was enjoying it all. I could see the finish line. A dream right before my eyes came true.

The divorce was final at the end of the year. I was now faced with some major financial responsibilities. I would have to work a second job to make ends meet. I wasn't planning on staying in Corona much longer. It was time to move forward. I don't know what I would have done without my mother.

Shortly after the divorce, I popped the big question to Cathy. Without any hesitation, she said, "*Yes!*" On June 1, 1985 I officially became a certified medical ultrasound technician. .It had taken a lot of hard work, dedication, and fortitude given the state of my life. I was very proud of myself. So were many, many others. My biggest fan and supporter was none other than my mother, Rosie. She uttered some words that I have been wanting to hear from her in a lifetime. "I'm so proud of you, Frankie, and I love you very much."

Wow—a Hallmark moment! I still get the GOOSEBUMPS.

CHAPTER XIX

A QUEENS TALE: FROM A LAB COAT TO A BLUE COLLAR

I thought now would be an appropriate time now for the kids to meet Cathy. I had been telling the kids about her in little bits and pieces; I didn't want to blindside them. I could still see in their bright little eyes some apprehension. It was to be expected.

The plan was that Cathy would meet us at their favorite McDonald's, which happened to be in Elmhurst, her neighborhood. It would be a late Sunday morning. This was the usual routine for us.

The anticipation before that meeting was building. After all, it was a very pivotal moment. On that particular Sunday, it was a rather damp, dreary day. I told Cathy to be there around eleven thirty. We got there around eleven. The kids got their usual Happy Meals, I got my usual egg sandwich and coffee, and we headed to our favorite booth. The place was a little busy. The kid asked me what time she would be coming. I had my eyes glued to the door that she would be walking through. I had planned to give a wave, letting her know where we were sitting. It was like waiting for the main character to appear on stage for the first time in a Broadway show. She was always prompt, another similarity we shared.

At exactly eleven thirty she walked in the door with a hood on that was soaked from the rain. I waved her over and she sat next to me in the booth. I said to the kids, "Say hello to Cathy!" In unison they said, "Hi Cathy!" Cathy immediately replied, "It's so nice to meet you guys." The conversation was pretty generic. *How is school, what's your favorite subject, do you have a favorite toy? I hear you guys are big Yankee fans.* Stuff like that. I asked her if she wanted to eat something. She said that she was okay. There was good eye contact going on between her and the kids—in between them looking for their toys from the Happy Meals.

She stayed about forty-five minutes. I felt the general vibe level being, I thought, reasonably acceptable. Upon leaving, she stood up, extended her hand out to the kids and said, "It was great meeting you." She looked at me and said, "Talk soon!" I gave her a wink and said okay. She walked out the door she came into, put her hood up, and braved the horrible weather that was waiting for her. All and all It was a big relief for all of us.

I couldn't wait to ask the Big Question. "So what did you guys think?" Frankie answered first in his very mature manner, "She seems like a very nice person—and pretty too." Tanyanelle chimed in with a typical response in her manner, "Don't you think she is a little young?" I thought that was comical. It was so on point as to her little outspoken reputation. No harm done at all. It was a good laugh.

As my Mother and entire family really got to know Cathy, they absolutely adored her. Everyone made the observation that our relationship was a very natural thing. My family went on to say that I even looked much better. I gained weight and my nagging stomach problem was all but gone. We even made a trip upstate to Schenectady, so she could meet Aunt Jen. After that visit, Aunt Jen wrote me and Cathy two beautiful individual letters. She said that she was extremely happy for us and could quickly feel the chemistry. She wrote that we made a beautiful couple and she was so happy that we are happy. Cathy went on to love all of my family as well. It was inspiring for me to see. Poetry in motion.

I can also say that I was well-received by Cathy's family. Just as her grandfather was retired from the New York City Department of Sanitation, so were her two uncles. It was a big family with strong ties to the Sanitation Department. Cathy's father also happened to have worked for the same Teamster Union Local 282 that my brother Johnny worked for. They actually had mutual friends. The connections just kept on ticking and ticking.

Here I was, now a medical professional. I was still working nights at the hospital. I was updating my resume and had all intentions to apply for an ultrasound tech position there. I truly believed that my prospects were very good. But my life had been nothing but twists and turns, ups and downs, and decision-making. Why would anything change?

While still in Corona, one morning I went down to that beautiful black-and-white marble hallway entrance to get the mail. It was deja vu all over again. I remembered when I got the letter from the Cincinnati Reds. As I was sorting through our mail, I saw a letter with the return address that read, NEW YORK CITY DEPARTMENT OF SANITATION. What in the world would they want? I could not wait till I got upstairs. I sat down on the cold marble steps and ripped open the letter.

It said, "Congratulations. You are being considered for a position of sanitation worker with the New York City Department of Sanitation." I honestly thought I was hallucinating. I definitely had to read it more than once. It said I had to report to 25 Hudson. *Holy shit*, I was saying more than once as I made my way back up the steps. I remembered that I took the Sanitation test back in 1973. Evidently, the hiring list was frozen for twelve years. My original list number was 22,268. If that's not luck, I don't know what is.

Rosie wasn't home, so my first call was to Cathy who was at work. She could not believe the news. She said that she will tell her grandfather right away. Now my head was really spinning. I'd just had a lifetime dream come true of being a medical professional. Who ever had a lifetime dream of becoming a garbage man?

It didn't take long to convince myself what career path I should follow. That was after talking to all of my family, close friends, and of course Cathy's heavily influenced sanitation family. I knew there was nothing wrong with me medically, so the process should be a slam dunk. I reported to the medical. It was a long pretty intense day. I got flashbacks to my short-term Wall Street days of riding the subways. They still didn't agree with me. (No men's room needed, though.)

The next step would be to receive a starting date. I had no choice but to wait. Corona was definitely a blue-collar town. Mostly trade unions, construction workers, and civil-service workers. Growing up, there had been a very large number of sanitation workers in my neighborhood. The word on the street was that you could never go wrong with a union or civil-service job. So I had a good chance, early in life, to see what was a sound career choice, especially if you didn't have a college education. That was certainly the norm in Corona.

I finally got my notice. It was another twist that I didn't expect. Here we go again.

The letter said, *After completion of your medical exam results, it has been determined that you are hereby disqualified from being appointed as a sanitation worker. We thank you for your interest and wish you good luck in your future endeavors.*

It was confusing on two levels. First, they did not tell me why. Second, they did not tell me that I could appeal the decision.

Now I was really screwed. The first person I called was Cathy's grandfather, Cono. He said, "Let me make a few phone calls." It just so happened that Cono's brother, Carmine, was best friends with the President of the Sanitation Union. Okay, all sounded good. I could sense a little ray of hope. Cono called me back and said, "It's all taken care of. You should get another letter shortly with a starting date."

Wow, wow, and *how!*

Throughout my journey, you and I have witnessed that forever-reverberating refrain. *It's not what you know, it's who you know.* I guess now, the last time, would be the best time it came to fruition. On July 29, 1985 I officially became a sanitation worker. My mother used to call me a garbage man of course. I actually called myself, a "garbologist." I thought it sounded more distinguished and sophisticated. I still was a medical professional at heart.

I have always firmly believed that in the scope of things and life in itself, *It's not where you start, it's where you finish.* My journey has now come to an end. While defining all my setbacks along the way, I learned to embrace their challenges. It was indeed an education. A new journey began on November 2, 1985, as Cathy and I became husband and wife.

I will always remember my grandparents telling the story of their *long journey* in a large, uncomfortable, unhygienic ship from Italy in their quest for the American Dream. I often wonder what they were thinking as their ship slowly approached New York Harbor and Lady Liberty. Might have been something like, *Life, Liberty, and the Prosciutto of Happiness!*

The difference between my grandparents' journey and my own, was I had a free ride to that American Dream. They'd had to pay a hefty price by leaving their families and many loved ones oceans and miles behind. As I reflect on my journey, I see I have always been touched and inspired by the famous words of another man, who had the distinction, as I did, of being born Francis and called Frank. The greatest music legend of the twentieth century, Frank Sinatra, was a strong fabric in our lives growing up in Corona. So let the record show, to old blue eyes from a young green eyes, let me be frank and proudly say, "I did it my way."

Alterations To A Life Jacket

NO WORDS ARE ENOUGH. THIS PICTURE IS A TRUE EXAMPLE OF THEIR UNCONDITIONAL LOVE. IN SPITE OF ALL THEIR HARDSHIPS AND STRUGGLES, THEIR EXEMPLARY ACTIONS, SERVED AS A GUIDING LIGHT FOR ALL THEIR CHILDREN. WE WILL NEVER FORGET.

OUR BELOVED GRANDPARENTS ACROSS THE HALL. SO BLESSED TO HAVE HAD THEM IN OUR LIVES. COULD NOT IMAGINE LIFE WITHOUT THEM.

THIS IS ONE OF THE TOP MERIT AWARDS RECOGNIZED BY THE NEW YORK CITY DEPARTMENT OF SANITATION, I RECEIVED IN 1988. THAT'S A GOOD FRIEND OF MINE, AL RAHNER. HE RETIRED AS A CHIEF IN THE DEPARTMENT.

Alterations To A Life Jacket

THIS IS MY CERTIFICATE MADE POSSIBLE BY GRANDPA FRANK. THE COST OF THIS 15 MONTH PROGRAM IN 1985 WAS THREE THOUSAND DOLLARS. NOW IT'S A TWO YEAR PROGRAM RECOGNIZED AS AN ASSOCIATE DEGREE. IT'S COST IS CURRENTLY AROUND THIRTY FIVE THOUSAND DOLLARS.

THE UNFORGETTABLE, UNBELIEVABLE SISTER TEAM, ROSIE AND JOSIE. JUST TO THINK THAT THEY RAISED TWELVE KIDS BETWEEN THEM. THEY ARE THE TRUE "QUEENS" OF CORONA.

ANOTHER WONDERFUL LADY AND A OUTSTANDING HUMAN BEING. MY FATHER'S LAST REMAINING SIBLING, OUR DEAR AUNT JEN. STILL RESIDING IN SCHENECTADY NEW YORK. A FAVORITE AUNT GROWING UP AND STILL IS TODAY. A REAL WARRIOR IT'S BYOND GREAT TO HAVE HER IN OUR LIVES.

PRIMARILY DUE TO LOGISTICS, IT IS NOT VERY OFTEN THAT WE ARE ALL IN THE SAME PLACE AT THE SAME TIME. FROM LEFT TO RIGHT, OUR LATE BROTHER JOEY, ANTHONY, MARY ANNE, ME, MICHAEL AND JOHNNY. WHEN WE DO GET TOGETHER, IT IS MAGICAL.

SADLY, THIS IS THE LAST PICTURE TAKEN OF ME AND MY MOTHER. JANUARY 28, 2005

ACKNOWLEDGEMENTS

To my wife, Cathy: There are not enough words to express all the feelings I have for you. For the past thirty-five years there have been many peaks and valleys, many ups and downs, many happy and many sad moments. The constant is you have always been my confidant, my friend, and my partner. You have also been the rock of the beautiful family we have created. From the day you married me along with my two kids, your courage, your strength, and your continued support and tremendous amount of patience have been nothing short of exemplary. You gave me a second chance at life. You forever treated Frankie and Tanyanelle as they were your own. They proudly loved you for that. You now treat my grandchildren just the same. It has been a testimony to see the outpouring of love. For the three intelligent, beautiful children you have given me and the unconditional love you constantly show, I'm beyond grateful. I pledge my continued love and admiration to you and us for another thirty-five years.

My three kids have each played an integral part in the making of this book. My English teacher, Amanda, put me on the right track as far as the content and structure of my writing strategies. She instilled in me the importance of not only telling the story, but of showing it. Monica gave me a quick education in the navigation of Google Docs and Microsoft Word. She is truly a wiz when it comes to the computer. She had to have a lot of patience with my not being computer savvy. I would constantly ask her questions—literally day and night. Jason, for Father's Day, bought me a book titled *How to Write the First Draft of Your Memoir*, which was an enormous help in the entire process. It really opened my eyes and inspired me to be creative and write from my heart. I can't thank you guys enough for the tremendous love and support you showed me. Don't worry, I have no intentions to write about any new journeys.

To my siblings, Anthony, MaryAnne, Michael, and Johnny: I thank you too for all your love and support. To Thomas Aiello, who lived directly across the street from us in Corona: You basically saw and just about joined Marottas' childhood experience. You were always in our presence. We all loved you as if you were one of us. Rosie always called you her sixth son. I will never forget that day your dad Sal brought us to our first Yankee game. I'm proud and honored to still call you my dear friend. I also want to thank you for being my sponsor at confirmation. By the way, I still got the watch.

To my best friend for over fifty-five years, Anthony Gaeta: You have always been like a big brother to me. I thank you for your continued love and support in this project and in life. Anthony has walked down the same blocks, taken the same paths, and driven the same roads as I. Basically having the same upbringing, he can totally relate to my story. Not to mention that he witnessed a lot of it. He is also the biggest Yankee fan I know.

To a real Hero of mine growing up, Richie Rizzo. Richie is also a Vietnam War Veteran. I can't explain how proud I am of you being the special person you have always been. How you always protected and watched over me, like a big brother as a kid. I'm forever grateful. To top it all you remain a HERO to us all, when you put your life on the line for our GREAT COUNTRY. I'm proud to also still be in contact with Richie as he and his Wife Kathy now reside in florida.

To my seasoned award winning Author friend Dennis Griffin, you gave me the vision and inspiration to write my story. In its beginning stages when you first read it, you said, "keep on writing, you most definitely have something special here"! I'm extremely grateful. To my many good friends, coworkers, cousins, nephews, nieces brother-in-law, sons-in-law, daughter-in-laws, mother-in-law, my last remaining wonderful Aunt Jen, you have all been an inspiration. Along with all your support, encouragement and compassion, will always be cherished, with much gratitude.

EPILOGUE

The year now is 2020. It needs no introduction. The" COVID-19 pandemic" will suffice. A rather odd and ironic fact was it was also called the *coronavirus*. The Corona, Queens zip code, 11368, was the most heavily concentrated hit area of the virus recorded in the City Of New York. By no means was the virus named after Corona. I just thought it was all quite interesting. Quarantine became a way of life for all of us. You can say that this book was my silver lining. I lost my job on March 20, 2020 and had nothing but time. So for the next five months, I spent close to ten hours a day writing in a notebook then transferring it all to a laptop.

I retired from the New York City Department of Sanitation in 2005, after exactly twenty years of service. My last day was to be on May 5, 2005. I never saw it. My mother, dear Rosie, passed away suddenly, on May 4, 2005. She was seventy-nine.

I worked in my old neighborhood, Corona, for a period of time. It was very gratifying and nostalgic, picking up the garbage pails I'd seen as a kid. I was able to have a pretty good nonconventional career. You would associate picking up household trash as the norm. I guess coming into the department with a rather educated professional background helped. I spent time in administration, training and development, and in the department of trial processing. I was also the resident writer for my district. I had quite a few stories published in the New York newspapers.

The time I was actually on the truck, two men would pick up thirteen tons a day of trash every day. Most sanitation departments put three men on a truck. Today, I experience chronic back pain as a result, not to mention the many other bodily pains and sprains. We worked in all extreme-weather conditions. The coldest day I ever worked was a temperature of seven degrees below zero, and the hottest was 107 degrees. It was tough. I must say it was all worth it, though, when I see my pension check every month along with having one-hundred percent medical coverage for me and my family.

After I retired from sanitation, I started another career in security for the biggest health system on Long Island. I retired after seventeen years. I now work part time for a major private university on Long Island, driving a campus shuttle. It keeps me busy while getting me out of the house.

Cathy and I were able to purchase our first home on Long Island in 1993. It was made possible by the wonderful generosity of our two families. It was always a struggle, financially, for us, as I always worked two jobs. Plus I always had my child-support obligations along the way. Again, it was well worth it—with no regrets. I remember the real-estate lady said that it would be a great "starter home." Twenty-seven years later, we are still here. We are very fortunate to have raised our three kids here.

Amanda lives with her husband Adam and my little bundle of joy, Roman, in Westchester County. We are extremely delighted to have Jason and my daughter-in-law Jenna ten minutes away with their new little Vincent, as they recently purchased their first home. Monica still lives at home with Mom and Dad. We are very proud of her many accomplishments and her musical talents as well. Amanda is a high-school English teacher here on Long Island. Jason is a medical specialist for Geico Insurance. Monica is an American Sign Language Interpreter and teacher's assistant in a special school for the deaf on the North Shore of Long Island.

Frank Jr. has had an illustrious career as an electrical-design engineer in the automotive industry. He has worked for Mercedes Benz, Tesla, General Motors, and presently Harley Davidson. I always knew his love and passion for cars would someday pay off. His career has taken him and his family to four different states. He is also an accomplished Musician. He currently performs with his singer-songwriter wife, Anne Heaton, and has performed all over the country. Frank and his family presently live in Wisconsin. If any son could be all a parent could ever hope for, I am proud beyond words and blessed to say I have a special star. We still have a really great, close relationship.

Tanyanelle had a promising career in the retail-food Industry until it was curtailed by a major back injury. She is now a stay-at-home mom and lives with her husband Ben and two daughters in a small town in Pennsylvania.

As for my siblings, Anthony is retired from Delta Airlines and lives in Upstate New York. MaryAnne works part-time as a school monitor and spends a lot of time, along with her husband, babysitting her two beautiful twin granddaughters. She has a heart of gold. She inherited many good traits from our mother, especially putting others first. She even looks like Rosie now. She lives in Queens, New York. John, always known as "one of the twins"! Lives Upstate New York with his wife Anita in the same town as Anthony. John is a proud retired Teamster. He and Anita have raised six children. They also spend a lot of time with their grandchildren. At the end of this year, they are expecting three more. Michael is living his dream. Over the last year he had a guest role in a popular Emmy-winning comedy series. Had a lead spot of an International pharmaceutical commercial. Just before the pandemic, he had a featured role in a promising off-Broadway show. He has indeed made the entire Marotta family proud. He lives with his partner Tony, just outside of New York City.

As for yours truly, the simple life suits me just fine. Some peace of mind and a little piece of the pie. I always wanted my own home, a nice car, and some financial stability. Above all, good health. With much confidence, I can say I did pretty good. THAT'S ALL SHE WROTE FOLKS!

www.ingramcontent.com/pod-product-compliance
Ingram Content Group UK Ltd.
Pitfield, Milton Keynes, MK11 3LW, UK
UKHW022237230426
12048UKWH00018BA/1310